NORMAN
the
DOORMAN

NORMAN
the
DOORMAN

THE SECRET TO A WORRY-FREE FINANCIAL LIFE

DAN MILLER

The Money Strong Creed ™ is a registered trademark
of MillerOnMoney.com

Published in the United States by Wild Owl Press,
Walnut Creek, CA.

www.wildowlpress.com

Books are available in special editions, for bulk purchases and for
corporate use. For more information call 925-977-3400 or email
info@wildowlpress.com

This book is sold with the understanding that neither the author
nor the publisher is engaged in rendering legal, accounting, or any
other professional service by publishing this book. As each situation
is different, all questions relevant to personal finances and specific to
the individual should be addressed to the appropriate professional
to ensure that the situation has been evaluated carefully and
appropriately. The author and publisher specifically disclaim any
liability, loss, or risk which is incurred as a consequence, directly or
indirectly, of the use and application of any of the contents of this
work. The characters in this book are fictional and are meant to
convey the concepts contained herein. Any similarity to real people,
lives, or events is unintended and coincidental.

Library of Congress Cataloging-in-Publication Data
Miller, Dan
Norman the Doorman: The Secret to a Worry Free Financial
Life/Dan Miller
1. Financial security   2. Personal finance   I. Title
ISBN 978-1-7362991-0-4
Ebook ISBN 978-1-7362991-1-1
Book design by Clare Baggaley
First Revised Paperback Edition

Library of Congress Control Number:
2021904443

Designer: Clare Baggaley www.clarebaggaley.graphics

Editor: Lisa Edwards

ABOUT THE AUTHOR

As an entrepreneur, mentor, and coach, Dan Miller has spent over thirty years helping individuals, families and businesses reduce financial anxiety and stress in their lives. Using simple strategies and straightforward advice, Dan guides people to take control of their finances and to build a stronger, more secure life. Dan has been asked to speak on the subjects of success, sales, personal finance, and business management by over 100 organizations and has coached over 12,000 people to achieve greater success. Happily married with a wonderful daughter, son-in-law and two perfect grandkids, Dan lives with his wife in the San Francisco Bay Area.

"What's missing from our kids' education and absent from most family dinner table discussions is how to successfully confront one of the most important challenges in life; how to become truly financially secure and create a shield from inevitable economic downturns. Dan Miller has written a book that engagingly describes a pathway to wealth and financial security that is guaranteed to work. Unlike other self-help books, Mr. Miller's advice is at once profound, simple to understand and easy to implement. And unlike many other authors, Mr. Miller practices what he preaches. This is required reading."

Curt Berrien, President, Berrien O'Brien Inc.

"Financial literacy is a central part of a successful life in today's world, yet only one-third of young adults possess it. Dan Miller, an expert, addresses this gap in this delightful tale, weaving in the core principles which allow one to become and remain financially secure. A must read!"

Dr. David B. Zenoff, counselor on strategy and management, former member of the faculties of Columbia & Stanford Graduate Schools of Business, author or co-author of nine books on management

"Norman the Doorman shows that a life of simplicity can create a life of abundance. Living by Norman's Money Strong Creed can help you build the financial life you want and protect you from difficult times. This is a powerful book with an important message about freedom, status, and how to have a strong self-concept despite the temptations that surround us."

Lull Mengesha, Author, Fintech for Social Impact

Weaver was the kind of town where people looked out for each other, walked to church on Sunday in their best clothes despite the weather, and brought their favorite family recipes to the big Fourth of July picnic in Prospect Park to share every year.

Even though the town wasn't far away from two big cities, it was just far away enough. It provided a simpler, less costly lifestyle, but Weaver's families could still overstuff a vehicle and make a day out of shopping and doing other big-city things without much difficulty.

The oldest streets in Weaver led directly to the park square at the center of town. The stately houses nearest the square with sweeping, manicured yards and motor courts looked very impressive, while the more modest homes with leaded-glass windows and wide, welcoming front porches further out were cared for and comfortable. Even the largest homes were far more affordable than either of the larger cities nearby, adding to Weaver's attraction to home buyers more recently.

Just outside of town, at the end of the grid of streets that had been laid since the days horses and buggies came through, there were groups of homes built around the time that the factories were converted to help aid the war effort many years before. These were mostly tidy cinderblock structures on streets named after influential local families or the children of the builders, each home looking just about identical to the others. Driving still further would show off the rolling hillside pastures and farmlands that connected little towns all over this area to one another.

Factory work fired the town's engine, just as it had for over one hundred years. Weaver was very lucky, luckier than most towns like it that had seen their factories fight for their lives as the world shifted around them, only to leave for good over time. Instead, Weaver prospered, partly due to good fortune and mostly due to its ability to find new uses for its assembly lines when the world changed around it. After high school, most people found a job at one of the town's three factories and started families, usually with someone they had known they would be with all their lives.

On Second Street, on the north side of the square heading out of town, two families lived next door to each other in houses that had originally belonged to distant relatives.

One of the homes was a Victorian, painted colorfully, while the other was a more conservative Craftsman, trimmed in a deep forest green. Both homes sat back comfortably from the street behind a sidewalk, and each home featured a walkway leading to front porches rimmed with potted plants.

A young boy named Bertram lived with his three older siblings in the Craftsman. Bertram was in perpetual motion, and he often couldn't be bothered to eat, which explained both his smaller stature and his mother's constant attempts to feed him something. He was fiercely competitive, especially with his two brothers, and didn't let his size, age, or any potential hazard distract him from attempting to win any and all possible challenges.

Next door, Bessie lived with her parents and a cat in the Victorian. Bessie's mom, a tall woman with dark hair who never seemed to notice that she looked like an Italian movie star, was one of the few people on the street who hadn't grown up in Weaver. She'd met Bessie's dad in Sicily while he was on shore leave and eventually traveled the thousands of miles to join him as his wife. Without other children in the house, Bessie spent much of her time with her mother, and when she shooed Bessie outside, with Bertram and his brothers and sister.

Despite their personality differences, Bertram was completely in love with Bessie. Bessie giggled at Bertram's antics, amused in that anxious way that suggests it might be fun to watch someone else get into trouble, and was perfectly happy when Bertram would provide a scene-by-scene description of a game she had just witnessed him play, cheering him on again at the right parts of the story.

On late evenings, as the summer started to fade, they would sit together on a bench or on the ground, watching the fireflies announce the nightfall, one of the only waking moments that Bertram could stay quiet and still, stealing sideways peeks at Bessie's profile as it lit up in little flashes.

Like many neighbors in town, Bertram and Bessie's parents were longtime friends. Their fathers, Sam and Roger, grew up on the opposite side of town and were one year apart but played football together on Weaver High's last all-state football team. Since then, the city's football prospects had never caught up to expectations, making that winning season sort of legendary, especially since Friday night high school football was just about as important as church to most folks and one of the primary sources of weekend entertainment.

Even though they had both been promoted at the factory over the years, Sam and Roger both continued to live their lives like they weren't getting management wages, saving the extra money for later instead of spending it freely. Most people in Weaver did the same—it was very uncommon to see brand-new cars or anything flashy anywhere in town, even at the Golf and Tennis Club, where Weaver's small group of wealthy business owners and professionals all socialized. For the factory owners, it may have been a conscious choice to be careful not to flaunt any excess they had the good fortune to make in any given year, not just because it seemed disrespectful to the workers, but also because the next year could bring a thunderstorm or two. There had been enough financial ups and downs that Weaver's residents were thankful and frugal, and Sam and Roger were no exception.

By the time Bertram entered high school, it was clear that he had serious talent as a football player. He could play an entire game on both offense and defense without losing steam, taking full advantage of every moment he had on the field. He figured that he might even be good enough to play in college if he could make up for his height and weight with physical ability and skill.

Bertram's coaches had to convince him to spend the time needed to keep his grades up. He would ride pretty close to the line of getting put on academic probation and correct his grades just enough and at just the right time to avoid being benched for violating student athlete requirements.

Bertram was a huge part of Weaver High's first back-to-back winning season in decades and one of the primary reasons they were able to make the playoffs. It wasn't uncommon for him to have both the most yards rushing and the most tackles during the course of a game, and the other kids thrived on his pressure to perform. Moreover, the team's no-loss record during Bertram's sophomore year attracted scouts from some of the biggest football schools in the country, making it possible that one or more of the star players might get some play time at an iconic school.

For her part, Bessie was studious and a high academic achiever who didn't care much about the social or sports activities of the school. While Bessie excelled at all things academic, she was particularly talented as a writer and took quickly to languages, much like her mother. By the time she was in her senior year, she spoke French, Italian, and Spanish fluently and Greek conversationally, allowing her to read classic literature in its original language with ease. Her writing had won some local prizes and even some state awards, and when it came time to think about college, liberal arts schools from around the country rewarded her application with invitations to attend.

Bessie and Bertram remained close friends and spent some evenings together, but less frequently than when they were young, mostly because their interests were so different. During their junior and senior years, they would have barely seen each other if they didn't live next door, traveling in different circles as they did.

Bertram got about as much attention from colleges as Bessie, and he had his heart set on one of three of the big Midwestern football schools. Only one of those, the biggest state university in the region, offered him a full scholarship and a guaranteed spot on the team, so he decided that would be where he'd go. Bessie ended up going east as well, choosing a small, expensive, liberal arts school in Pennsylvania that didn't offer scholarship money, about as opposite a choice from Bertram's as one could make.

They saw each other only a few times during the last summer they spent at home, mostly as one was coming or going. Bertram was working part time at his uncle's hardware store to save some extra money and spending the rest of his time in the weight room and on the track. Bessie spent her mornings lifeguarding at the community pool and every other evening waitressing, hoping to do the same. Bertram didn't have many days between graduation and the start of team-conditioning practices, and he wanted to be sure to spend the little time he did have getting as prepared as possible. Bessie was planning to visit her mom's family in Sicily around the same time Bertram was scheduled to leave, so she was focused on putting away as much as she could for the trip, planning to tour around Europe a bit during the time she was there.

Finally, one early morning in July, it was time for Bertram to report to training camp; his father's four-door was so packed to the gills with stuff, there was barely enough room for Bertram left in the passenger seat. He was so preoccupied and excited, he almost forgot to say good-bye to his oldest brother and his mother. As he walked down the front walkway to where his dad had pulled around, he cast a glance toward

Bessie's still, dark house. He gazed up at her window and wondered if he should try to wake her to say good-bye, hesitating to knock.

Bertram was still thinking when he heard Bessie's screen door squeak open and saw her come out to the porch, already suited up for work at the pool with a WPD T-shirt and shorts and a red ball cap with a white cross emblazoned on it. He ran over to her, and they hugged silently for a minute. He pulled back, and her eyes were moist, which he had to admit made him smile. "Gonna miss you," he said in a half-whisper. She just nodded and tried to keep the tears back. "I hope we are home at the same time over the holidays," he said to fill space. Bertram's dad had started the car and now flicked the lights, needing to get him to his dorm in time to report.

"Bye," Bessie managed, pulling Bertram close again for a quick, firm hug.

"Bye," he shot back, grinning to lighten the mood. "Keep your eye on the sports page!" he joked as he backed away and then jogged back to the car.

Bessie waved as they pulled away, knowing that a lot would change for them both, and wondering how much they'd still have in common the next time they saw each other. A minute or so after the taillights were too far away to make out, she turned back to the house to start her day.

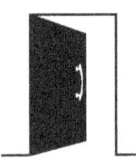

Bertram looked around his new office. The clean lines and monochrome colors made him feel important, as did the view out the window with a peek of the park and a solid shot of the river. Only four years out of college and he'd come a long way, getting promoted twice in a short period. Now he was in the big leagues, or at least it felt that way; assigned big-name accounts that even his parents had heard of, often dealing with higher-level executives who were twice his age. His competitive drive, which served him so well on the football field, translated perfectly into a sales position; in fact, the results came easily and he was often on top of the leaderboard for new business, despite his smaller territory and lack of experience.

Bertram also was well-liked by almost everybody, even though he had an intensity that could have come off as pushy in the wrong hands. Luckily, he also was quick with a compliment or an encouraging word and seemed to genuinely care about the people around him. He seemed to be in constant conversation and socialized well, building relationships that made him easy to promote, even over more senior people. On the rare occasion that he rubbed someone the wrong way, he could usually get back in their good graces if given the chance.

When he first moved to the city, he'd lived with roommates but that had quickly gotten old. He found that he was focused on his career and they were more interested in late-night partying than he was. Once he could barely afford it, he found an apartment not that far from the office that was tiny but quiet. It wasn't much, but it worked well enough and he stayed there for well over a year.

As he started to earn more, Bertram thought he should find something a bit more 'respectable' and looked for something in one of the new buildings downtown. He found an amazing two-bedroom place down by the newly redeveloped waterfront area and couldn't pass it up, even though the rent was twenty percent more than he was hoping to spend. He wanted to convey a certain image and this apartment seemed to fit that image like it was made to order. It even had a doorman – a tall African American man of indeterminate age with broad shoulders, an elegantly casual manner, and a mellifluous voice who greeted him with a warm smile when he came to tour the place.

Although the added expense made him nervous, with his newly increasing income, Bertram, figured he could grow into the extra cost. "Why not?" he said to himself out loud in his car as he pulled away. "I deserve this."

This was similar to a conversation he'd had with himself at the car dealership late the previous year when it became clear that he needed to replace his beat-up Toyota truck with something he could take a client to lunch in. He had initially been intending to replace the truck with a Camry but stopped at the BMW dealership next door on a whim. After making the mistake of sitting in one of the new feisty performance sedans, he found himself signing a purchase agreement for a glacier silver 330i and speeding off with the stereo blasting. He happened to be looking in the rearview when he saw one of the employees drive his trusty truck back towards the service and detail area. He felt a sharp pang as he heard his father saying, "That was a perfectly good working truck," in his mind, but he quickly shook himself clear of the unwanted invasion. As usual, Bertram wasn't one to dwell on things.

Bessie massaged a fugitive strand of hair to its confinement behind her ear as she pondered a sample lesson plan that was due later that week. It was early enough in the still-darkened morning that she chose to sit in the wingback chair in the living room; the lamp with the hummingbird lampshade offered warm light that wouldn't disturb her mom's slumber. The assignment had been to create a plan that integrated movement and collaboration into a mathematics lesson for a fictional third-grade class and she had come up with an idea that she felt pretty good about, if not completely confident in its potential for success. Putting down her pencil and notebook briefly, she tugged at the diamond-patterned afghan so that it covered her legs more completely. Bessie sat back in the chair so that her back bumped the buttons in the fabric, looking at the darkness of the living room where she had spent most of her life and envisioning the setting precisely even though the light wasn't strong enough to illuminate it. She allowed herself a moment to absorb her surroundings before bringing herself back to the task at hand, thinking about the unexpected path she had traveled and the journey still ahead. "Soon," she thought, "I will be teaching my friends' kids." Some of them had already had their first baby or even their second. While she was away at school, most of her high-school classmates stuck around, got jobs, got married and were working on their families. Bessie wanted kids of her own one day but wasn't ready for that now, and besides, she didn't have someone serious in her life.

After college, Bessie spent a summer in Italy intending to spend the year there, but an unexpected phone call brought her back home before her adventure could fully unfold. Roger, her larger-than-life father, capable of anything, had a serious heart attack and hadn't yet returned to consciousness. Her usually relaxed and confident mother was clearly emotionally fragile and Bessie immediately found a plane home to be by her side, and hoped her Dad would recover and that she could help in the meantime. Instead, somewhere after she caught her connection at Kennedy but before she landed in Chicago for the last leg of her trip, Roger passed away.

The next couple of months were hazy, even in Bessie's memory. She remembers helping her mom figure out the logistics of the funeral and other details, and how quiet the house was, especially on weekends when Roger's tools would usually be busily buzzing and whirring as he set about one project or another. Her mom's ever-present smile took a holiday and she slept until late in the morning. Bessie did her best to keep the household running, shopping, cooking and cleaning so her mother could process the loss, even though she was fighting through her own grief the whole time.

Later, it became clear that Bessie wasn't aware of their financial situation, which turned out to be more challenging than she could have anticipated. She figured that her parents had limited savings since they were still young – and her mom's regular output of small sculptures she sometimes sold at a gallery in town, while exquisitely artistic, didn't contribute much to the household income. What she was shocked and embarrassed to learn is that her parents took out a mortgage on the house to help fund her Swarthmore tuition and housing, some of which was paid for through academic scholarship, but most of which was not. Bessie's mom explained that they didn't want her to worry about money and that they only had one child so they wanted to help her live out her dreams.

The price of that was large, leaving a mortgage, a small amount of savings, and no income to speak of. The reality of the severity of the situation took a while to take hold, during which time Bessie had already enrolled in a teaching credential program available through the state college system. She had always thought that teaching might be a good fit and her desire for a stable, long-term career with a pension was underlined by the recent events in her life. She worked evenings at the same restaurant that helped her to fund her first visit to Europe years ago and it helped her to have both distractions.

Bessie's mom was slower to find a new normal which became more problematic as the savings dwindled. There wasn't much to begin with, but it got them through the first months without much difficulty. Then the mortgage company started calling and mailing, becoming more and more persistent about the money they owed. Bessie had even been taking to bringing home food from work as dinner, explaining to her mom that it was a 'perk' of the job, but not very convincingly.

Bessie had no idea what to do and just when she started to worry that she was going to have to try to convince her mom to sell the house so they didn't lose it, she woke up to a note: "Bess, I am going to Dad's factory to see about a job. See you at dinner…"

Bessie was wracked with guilt about the fact that her mother had to go to work to do something other than sculpting and that her fancy private college was a large part of the reason. She wished she could trade in her education, which was wonderful but not necessary, for the inexpensive state college where she was now earning her credential, knowing that she couldn't change the past. She felt unnecessarily spoiled and indulged which she had never considered before and even though her mother assured her that she was being silly when she tried to talk to her about it, she couldn't shake the feeling.

Fortunately, between the little bit extra Bessie made in weekend shifts at the café and her mother's factory wages, they were able to get the mortgage company to agree to a plan that allowed them to make smaller payments for a while until they got on their feet. Bessie learned to budget and made sure that neither she nor her mom ever spent an extra nickel. They lived simply and started to feel like the world wasn't going to spontaneously combust, at least not immediately. She resolved to take the financial stress as a lesson, promising herself that she would always put security at the top of the priority list, even when other things looked attractive or alluring.

Bertram moved into his new place on a Sunday in September, the week before the regular NFL season kicked off. The doorman, who introduced himself as Norman, was a saint, helping him load the last few things from the U-Haul into the freight elevator, and even helping him lug some of the heavier things into the apartment throughout the day. "Norman," Bertram said as he mopped his forehead with a kitchen towel he fished out of one of the boxes, "I don't know what I'd have done without you."

Norman smiled and thanked him. "It's my pleasure," he said, patting Bertram once on the shoulder with one of his massive hands and turning to leave.

"No really," Bertram scrambled to find his wallet. "Let me at least give you something..." Too late: Norman already was moving to the door, Bertram bustling after him with a wad of bills. "Seriously." Bertram shoved the ball of money towards Norman.

Norman opened the door and just smiled, shaking his head in a small but confident gesture, looking fresh and relaxed. "Bertram, you don't ever have to tip a friend." And he disappeared back into the hallway.

The following week, Bertram spent the evenings getting his new place put together. It became apparent that he was seriously in need of some new furniture; most of the few pieces he had looked like they'd come out of a storage locker in a fraternity house. After the rent and deposit, he didn't have much extra cash but was able to buy a number of things anyway since the couple of retailers he preferred offered a pretty sizable discount for signing up for their credit cards to finance the purchases. He figured he could pay most of the credit off with his annual bonus in January since his sales projections were strong, and anyway, he couldn't have a beautiful apartment without anywhere to sit. One slightly bigger splurge was a sixty-inch TV that had all the latest bells and whistles, a transgression easily justified in Bertram's mind by the hours during college and pro football that he and his friends would spend perched in front of it.

Bertram often bumped into Norman in the lobby and they had casual conversations, mostly about football. It turned out Norman had played high-school ball as an all-state defensive tackle, and was a less-avid NFL fan than Bertram but could still talk the game quite competently. Thinking about how much Norman had helped him, when he didn't even know him, Bertram asked Norman to come watch a game a few weeks into the season and they hung out for a couple of hours once his shift had ended.

Norman had a way of asking questions and remaining interested in the answer that accentuated Bertram's propensity to jabber. By the time the day was over, Norman knew details about the academic woes and poor choices that ended Bertram's football career and almost made it so he didn't finish college at all. He finally got it together enough to be released from academic probation to play the final four games of his final season of eligibility, but he had disappointed himself and his team. He mused that it was possible if he hadn't had been out for most of the in-conference games that year, they probably would have had a much better shot at the playoffs, and maybe even had a shot to go further. His coach, a tough ex-marine who played three seasons for the Minnesota Vikings before blowing out his Achilles and never quite recovering, threw every possible resource at Bertram. He yelled at him as much as he thought might be helpful but Bertram just wasn't willing to commit enough time to his studies. He loved to play football, but he was hard-headed enough to be his own worst enemy, choosing to skip classes and even tutoring sessions.

For his part, Bertram couldn't believe he had shared so much, or that Norman had patiently nursed a single glass of ice water while Bertram had more than a couple of beers and a half a bag of chips. Embarrassed at how messy his portion of the coffee table was, Bertram kidded, "What are you, some kind of Buddhist? You're making me look bad over here."

Norman laughed deeply. "No, no, Buddhists like to eat." Bertram cracked up. Norman shook his head. "No, I'm no Buddhist, but I have no intention of spoiling my dinner. Irma's been cooking with her sister all day and that can only mean gumbo is in my future."

Bertram had never had gumbo but the way Norman said it, he was sure that it must be unbelievable. "You're married?" Bertram's eyes shot to Norman's left hand which didn't have a ring on it.

"Yeah, hard to believe I could convince anyone to do it, huh?" Norman joked. "I can't wear rings, these big mitts of mine make them darn uncomfortable," he added, holding up his hands for inspection. They both laughed.

Norman checked the time and stood to go.

"Thank you so much for having me up, it's been great to get to know you." Norman grabbed a few of the empties and took a last sip of his water as he stood to leave, trashing the bottles in recycling and putting the glass in the dishwasher before Bertram could protest. They chatted for a few more minutes, agreeing to do it again sometime soon and Norman headed out looking as if gumbo might be at the forefront of his mind.

On a rare, quiet Sunday afternoon, Bessie was watching the snow fall from the living-room window. She'd just finished the book she had been devouring over the holidays and sipping a cup of too-hot tea when the phone rang. She figured her mom was upstairs in the studio and unfolded herself from the blanket she had wrapped around her legs. It was unusual to get calls on the house phone since almost anyone they knew would call their cellphones directly and the sound was startling. Bessie figured it was a telemarketer and let the message machine click on, but listened as it recorded. The caller was from the HR department at the factory and was looking for her mom; she picked up as soon as she realized who it was but the line had already gone dead. Something about the unexpected Sunday call felt ominous and she went to find her mother.

Bessie's mom was cleaning up in the little powder room next to the bedroom she used as her art studio. She smiled warmly as she dried her hands and looked at her daughter, a smile Bessie hadn't seen in quite some time.

"Hey, mom. Someone from Human Resources at work called and left a message on the landline. It sounded like something important but I didn't pick up in time." Her mom's face shadowed like a cloud had blown in between them. "What's going on? Bessie asked, nervously fiddling with a couple of the glazing brushes that were drying on the counter.

Her mom paused and then shrugged slowly. "It's probably a layoff. I've been hearing people talking about it in the accounting department. One of the big clients we work with has taken their work overseas and we haven't been able to replace it yet."

Bessie tried to hide her alarm, she knew they were just barely making ends meet with the new adjusted payment on the mortgage and she wasn't sure how they would survive without her mom's income. Her mom gracefully motioned her towards the stairwell and they walked down to the kitchen in silence.

Bessie heard her mom's side of the conversation from the living room. The news wasn't good but it didn't sound like she had lost her job completely. Her mother sounded as if she was consoling the HR person instead of the other way around, which didn't mean much since it was typical of how she operated in every circumstance. She remembered her mom comforting her father's brother at the memorial service, holding him close and assuring him that Roger loved him, even though she was broken inside herself. Bessie heard her mother filling a pot of water and went in to find out what had happened.

She didn't really want to ask since the answer was likely to be scary. "So… what did they say?"

Her mom went to the pantry and pulled out a couple jars of the tomatoes she had canned that summer, almost a lifetime before. "They are doing a large layoff. I'm lucky… They only reduced my hours to part-time so at least I still have a job. But lots of people weren't so lucky," she answered as she removed the tops of the jars and set the tomatoes to drain.

Bessie could feel her heart beating in her head. "How many hours will you still get a week?" Bessie was already doing multiple math scenarios in her head… If it was less than thirty, they couldn't pay the bills.

"They're giving me twenty hours through the springtime, maybe more if they can get a new client on board. Bessie, I know you're worried, but we'll figure it out." Her mom turned to face her. "You are too young to have to worry about this… You're almost done with your credential and then you can start teaching, which will solve the problem."

Bessie exhaled, appreciating her mom's optimism and attitude while knowing it was misplaced at the same time.

"We can sell the house. We would get some money after paying off the mortgage and that could keep us going until you start working. By that time, I should be back full-time as well," her mom said, as if she was suggesting adding more onions to her tomato sauce.

Bessie considered that thought. The problems with this idea were practical. First, it was the dead of winter and no one tended to buy houses during the winter. Added to that the fact that a good portion of the town would be affected by the layoff and it seemed unlikely that it would be possible to sell the house at all until everyone was working again. They earned just enough money each month to pay all the bills, usually juggling one or two if possible; there was no way they could survive on less. Bessie could quit the credential program but that didn't really help either since she already had paid her final tuition and she couldn't earn enough money taking more shifts at the café to make up the difference anyway. They had already gotten the mortgage company to adjust their payment and it wasn't likely that they could get any more relief there and they shared one older car that somehow continued to putter them around without incident. There wasn't anywhere left to save that could make enough of an impact to make up for her mom's lost income.

Bessie could only see one option. "Mom, we can put the house up for sale but I'm not sure we will be able to sell it. We might have to stop making payments. If we do that, the bank will foreclose on us." Bessie was fighting back tears. "I don't know what to do…" she sobbed as her mom wrapped her arms around her and rocked her side to side like she did when she was a little girl.

"It's going to be ok, Bess. We'll figure it out, I promise."
Bessie was doubtful but her mom's warm body and calm
confidence always was soothing and she let her shoulders relax
as she returned the hug.

— — —

Bertram was early for his annual sales-planning meeting with
Mr. Vaughan, his supervisor, and thought he'd take a spin
around the office. Not too many people had straggled in yet
from the weekend and the snowy weather made it likely that it
would be a pretty light day, which wasn't Bertram's preference.
He thrived on the energy when everyone was in full swing
and felt at a loose end when there wasn't electricity in the air.
Even after a huge football weekend and hosting a big party
at his apartment with his two best friends to watch the NFC
championship game, he was ready for action. He was excited
to talk about his plan for the year and maybe even more so to
learn what his bonus was going to be based on his prior year's
performance.

Mr. Vaughan was a good boss but a tough one, a man of
few words who expected performance and didn't hang out
with his team like some of the other executives. His four kids
all had kids of their own which kept him occupied out of
work and he was a seriously committed golfer. Outside of that,
he didn't have many obvious interests and he seemed a little
enigmatic. Bertram found him more challenging to work for
than both of his previous bosses since developing relationships
came easily to him, usually using drinks and steak dinners as a
way to build some rapport, neither of which was part of Mr.
Vaughan's *modus operandi*. Mr. Vaughan was serious and sober,
starting and ending meetings on time with little patience for
personal conversation.

"Hey Bertram!" His buddy Paul flagged him down as he
was walking back toward Mr. Vaughan's office.

"Hi, Paul, how was your holiday?" Bertram gave his friend a big hug. Paul had spent the New Year and the first week of January on vacation with his wife and two kids in the Caribbean and his normally pasty-white skin looked like a worn baseball mitt with the exception of the sunglasses outlined on his face.

"Thanks! It was awesome. Super to get a break from the snow cone we've been living in for the past couple of months."

Mr. Vaughan stepped off the elevator and nodded his greeting with a firm-lipped smile to both as he walked by, heading to his office. "Hi, Paul, glad you're back. See you in a few minutes, Bertram?" he tossed out as he went by.

"Yes, sir," Bertram responded, a little too cheerily.

"Annual sales review time, right?" Paul asked knowingly.

Bertram nodded. "Ready for my big bonus for crushing it last year," he said in reply.

"Yeah, you had a great year," Paul agreed, "but don't be surprised if it's not what you expected."

Bertram was visibly startled. He'd been counting on that bonus; in fact, he'd factored his estimate of what it would be into a lot of his decisions, including his move uptown and a number of purchases around the house. "What do you mean?"

"Well... I had my conversation with Mr. Vaughan before I left on vacation and it didn't go as planned. Based upon how far over goal I was, I had expected the top-tier payout. Turns out, they moved the goalposts and never told us. I got half what I thought I was going to get."

Bertram was trying to process what he was hearing. "So, what did you say? That doesn't make sense."

"What could I say?" Paul shrugged. "Vaughan said that corporate wasn't approving bonuses over the second tier because the company didn't meet its projected profit numbers. He's never very detailed and I didn't push it." Paul checked his watch. "Hey, you're going to be late."

Bertram thanked him again and tried to get his head together as he walked down the hall. If the bonus was half what he was expecting, he wouldn't be able to pay off any of the purchases he'd made to furnish the apartment, not to mention that he would have almost nothing in savings since he'd spent so much between the move, getting the place furnished and his active social life. Being so close to expensive bars and restaurants hadn't seemed like anything but a benefit before, but now as he took a hard swallow to steady himself, he wondered if he may have misjudged their value.

Mr. Vaughan looked up over his black reading glasses and motioned Bertram to a seat. "Good holiday?" he asked, without losing track of the spreadsheet he was marking up.

"Yes, thanks, it was nice," Bertram responded, resisting the nagging urge to elaborate. He sat looking around the office. It had a few pictures of family and one plant that looked like it may have been fake but it was hard to tell. Typically, Bertram would pop up and rub a leaf to confirm but he didn't have that kind of relationship with Vaughan and thought better of it.

After what seemed like a century, Mr. Vaughan pushed his papers in a folder, clipped them together and stuck the folder in a stand-up at the corner of his desk. He turned to his credenza and took out two copies of what looked to Bertram like a sales projection and handed him one. "The first page is a goal versus actual comparison for your personal results last year. The second page is your team's version of the same data. Since you took over your new position, I thought we should look at both. How do you think last year went for you?"

Bertram broke away from the data to meet his gaze. "I had a great year. As you can see, I grew the territory by thirty percent and I exceeded the annual goal both personally and for the team." Bertram pointed to the numbers on his page.

Mr. Vaughan was nodding. "I agree, you had a good year. Your personal production is in line with the other territory managers but I think you could've done more. Territory growth in your prior year was stronger and I think you've had a hard time adjusting to the dual function of managing your clients and now managing a small team. This year, we're going to raise the bar." Vaughan flipped to the next page and Bertram did the same, trying to tamp down the brewing impulse to defend himself. "Here's what this year needs to look like," Vaughan continued. "Thirty-five percent personal territory growth and thirty-five percent team growth."

Bertram couldn't contain himself. "Those numbers are too big, the territory is mature and we've only got three of us covering it. I assume I can hire a few people to get us there?"

"No. We're in cost-containment mode, this should be possible with your existing team," Vaughan shot back.

Bertram pushed back in his chair. He was boiling a little inside and was not used to feeling like he wasn't achieving what was expected. How was it possible that he blew through his goals and that wasn't enough? Moreover, how was he going to get his tiny team to achieve the unrealistic numbers that Mr. Vaughan was asking for? While he was still thinking about how to respond, Mr. Vaughan flipped to the final page.

"For last year, you achieved tier-one bonus so you can expect that amount on your next paycheck," he said as if reading scripture.

Bertram's mouth dropped open. Paul was right, he was getting a little less than half what he was expecting. "I don't understand, I hit tier three not tier one," he said through gritted teeth.

"No, actually, you hit tier one. Take a look at your revised compensation agreement. When you went from a territory manager to a sales manager, your tier values changed. It's all in there." Mr. Vaughan pulled out the document that Bertram didn't even recall signing and pointed at the appropriate section.

Bertram read it and sat still for a moment, the severity of the situation burning in his gut. "If I had understood that I never would have taken the position on. This is crazy. I earned that bonus. Why would I take a promotion and make less money? That's stupid!" Bertram's voice rose.

"Bertram," Mr. Vaughan said calmly, "sit down."

Bertram had gotten out of his seat and was yelling loudly enough that people outside Vaughan's office were looking inside with concern. Bertram slowly talked himself into the seat, seething.

"Look, your new position came with a nice increase and the combination of that, plus the tier-one bonus is actually more than if you had your prior salary and the tier-three bonus. I'm sorry you're surprised by it, but you shouldn't be. It's there in your agreement and HR went over it with you in August when you made the move. This year, you can make big money, just achieve the growth goals," Mr. Vaughan said.

Bertram didn't respond which was probably a wise decision since he could be a real hothead and didn't want to get himself fired on top of it all.

"Ok, thanks for coming in," Mr. Vaughan was standing and put out his hand. "I know you can do this and this will be a big year. Don't let this get in the way."

Bertram stared at Vaughan's hand and eventually shook it more firmly than necessary, managing a single tense nod before stalking off.

Bertram was a few minutes late meeting his friend Simon for a cocktail. He shrugged off his heavy coat and gave his personal pile of winter protection to the petite woman at the coat check, along with his most winning smile, which she returned. He found Simon at the crowded bar and squeezed in next to him, flagging down the bartender as he did so. "Hey buddy," he said, shaking Simon's hand. "Sorry I'm late."

Simon looked like he'd been there a while, his staple vodka tonic down to a few cubes of ice and a lemon twist. "No problem, gave me a chance to warm up," he replied.

The bartender dropped Bertram's drink along with a refill for Simon. "Yeah, it's been a rough winter and we're aren't even halfway through yet," Bertram said, clinking glasses with his friend and taking a big sip of his cocktail.

Simon raised his eyebrows and motioned his head towards Bertram's glass. "Rough day?" he asked, knowing that Bertram was more of a beer lover than a hard-liquor guy.

Bertram nodded and took another sip of his Manhattan. "For sure," he responded.

"Want to grab a table? I'm starving," Simon suggested.

Bertram hesitated for a moment, thinking that he had no business spending big dollars on a steak dinner since his bank account was running on empty already, considering whether he should suggest the cheaper Chinese spot around the corner that he frequented on weeknights. "Sure, why not?" he said instead.

Simon and Bertram had roomed together during freshman year in college and been close friends ever since. All the student athletes at school roomed in the same hall and Simon was a starter on the basketball roster even though he was only a freshman. Simon was one of those basketball players who made everything on the court look easy, looking like he'd been born with a ball in his hands. His court persona matched his personal approach to just about everything, making him practically the opposite of Bertram who could never relax and had to work like a devil just to stay on par with his teammates. Simon was also a solid student who never seemed to study but got decent grades, which Bertram could only marvel at as he struggled with every subject.

Right after college, Simon had gotten a job in California

but had recently moved back east and happened to work two blocks from Bertram's office, making it possible for them to hang out pretty regularly. The only hitch was that Simon had a serious girlfriend who occupied most of his attention, while Bertram continued his now well-honed approach of dating multiple women while avoiding any commitment.

Moving downtown had been a big lift for Bertram's social life, making it easy for him to date or bar hop without ever needing a car or a cab and the restaurants all knew him by name. "Hey Lisa," Bertram greeted their server as she smiled at him and took their entrée orders. "How's it going?"

"It's great. This cold weather means that no one ever leaves once they get here, and they seem pretty thirsty," she responded with a wry smile. They all chuckled. "Another?" she asked, motioning towards his empty glass.

"Sure," he said.

Lisa took the empty and disappeared into the sea of bar patrons. Their entrées came fairly quickly and they had finished their typical rants about the NFL playoffs and other mostly sports-related topics.

"What's up with you, man? You seem a little distracted," Simon asked after Lisa came back to check on them again.

"What do you mean?" Bertram said little defensively.

"Well… there's no planet on which you wouldn't have gotten her phone number already if you were your normal self," he said smiling, his eyes directed at Lisa who was chatting with some guests at a table closer to the bar. "You're off your game for sure."

Bertram leaned back and ran his hand through his hair, sighing a little. He was trying to decide what he wanted to share with Simon – he wasn't really comfortable talking about money, especially when it would point out that he had none. He coughed. "I just found out that the bonus I was expecting and earned for last year is going to be a lot less than it was supposed to be," he said, editing out the distress that fact had caused on his financial picture.

"Oh, that's definitely a bummer," Simon acknowledged, finishing the last of his steak.

"Yeah, I'm pissed about it," Bertram retorted, not able to hide his residual anger. Simon nodded as if to empathize and also invite him to continue if he wanted to. "I... well, moving was expensive and I had calculated the numbers based upon what they owed me," Bertram explained, still reticent to share the total picture.

"That apartment is pretty amazing, no way I could swing that rent even if Melinda and I moved in together," Simon offered.

"Really?" Bertram asked in surprise. He figured that Simon was making at least the same money as he was.

"For sure. I mean, the place I'm in now is fine. I'm saving a bunch so that maybe I can buy a house and I don't really need much space. The fact is, I'm barely ever home except to sleep or hang with Melinda."

Bertram chewed on that for a moment. "I entertain a fair amount and needed the extra space, plus I'm earning plenty of money and wanted to reward myself," Bertram justified. "I love that place and it's right by the office," he added. Simon nodded and didn't respond. "Anyway, I'll figure it out. It was just a tough day, that's all."

Lisa came back to pick up the check. Simon insisted on buying and Bertram didn't argue too forcefully, somewhat relieved. They collected their coats, scarves and hats from the coat-check area and gave each other a hug just outside the door, preparing to go their separate ways.

"Ask Melinda if you guys can make the Super Bowl party this year... It's going to be awesome!" Bertram yelled as they went their separate ways.

"Isn't it always?" Simon responded, having experienced

Bertram's immortal parties in the past. They waved and trudged off into the snowy night.

———

A few weeks later, Bertram shook the snow off his jacket on a blustery Saturday after a not-so-great date at a new place around the corner. Despite his best efforts, Bertram couldn't really get into the conversation even though his date was both attractive and interesting; usually he would have happily and successfully turned on his magic. Not this night. It was all he could do to stop thinking about the size of the pending check and his mounting financial problems.

"Bertram," the deep voice came from the storage area behind the elevators.

"Norman?" Bertram asked tentatively. "Where are you?" He peered around the corner just as Norman's towering figure emerged.

"Good evening!" Norman greeted him with a pat on the shoulder as he emerged. "I haven't seen you in a few days. Is everything ok?"

"I'm good, thanks, Norman," Bertram responded, a bit unconvincingly. "Just been busy at work lately. How's it going with you?" he responded, hoping to change the subject.

"I'm great, thanks. Looking forward to seeing spring weather though. These big creaky dinosaur joints of mine aren't too fond of the cold." He patted his hips with a barely perceptible little shimmy to illustrate. Bertram chuckled. "I'm glad I caught you. Irma and I were talking and we'd love to have you over to take a taste of that gumbo I've blabbered about. Do you have a Sunday free that could work?" Norman asked warmly.

"Sure, wow, I mean, yes thanks, that would be great. It might be a few weeks... I think I'm booked for the next few Sundays. Maybe three Sundays from now?" Bertram checked his phone for a conflict and they sorted out a date that worked.

———

"I noticed your social calendar stays quite full so I thought I'd ask well in advance," Norman chuckled, recalling just having assisted a too-tipsy young lady in finding a ride home after the Super Bowl party recently, when she couldn't figure out her ride-sharing app. "Yes, that's perfect. I'll let Irma know."

"Ok great. Please thank her for me… Is there anything I can bring?" Bertram offered.

"No, no, please just come as you are. We'll be thrilled to have you."

Bertram got the address and put it in his calendar. "Thanks again, Norman. Looking forward to meeting Irma," Bertram signed off distractedly and headed up to his apartment.

Bessie got to the city about an hour early. She wanted to settle her nerves a bit and always found driving and parking in the city to be extremely distressing, so she had given herself plenty of time. Her appointment was in the tall glass building across the street from the garage but there was a coffee shop next to the entrance and she decided to order a green tea and see if she could bring herself to relax a little.

She had sat down with her mom and showed her exactly how bad their financial picture was, not wanting to keep her in the dark, but also hoping not to scare her. Her mother's reaction shouldn't have surprised her; she calmly listened to all of the details and asked a few questions, smiling wistfully at the end of it all.

"You did such a nice job of explaining all of that," she said, gazing fondly at her daughter.

Bessie blushed and thanked her but tried to get her attention on the reality: they were flat broke. There wouldn't be enough money to pay the revised mortgage payment next month which meant the bank could take possession of the house. Typically, banks had a long process they were required to go through but in this case, since they allowed a restructured payment plan, they were able to speed that up if they wanted. Once they stopped paying they'd soon be homeless.

In one last ditch effort, she thought she'd go and talk to the bank personally, since they had recently moved their corporate office to the city and Weaver was only an hour and half or so away. She knew it was a long shot but she thought it was worth a try. Now, though, seated with her steaming tea that she couldn't afford and looking out the window at the bustling street and the bank looming in the background, she wasn't so sure. A couple of tears had escaped from her attempts to restrain them and she dabbed at her eyes. "Pull yourself together Bessie," she said under her breath, which didn't seem to help. She wasn't used to wearing makeup and hoped that it was still in its proper place, fishing for a compact to double check. As she swung her head back up to investigate the makeup situation, a man was standing before her, offering a linen handkerchief.

"Are you ok, miss?" the tall, well -dressed man asked softly, with genuine concern."Oh, yes. Thank you." Bessie tried to shake off her emotions and look as if she was, in fact, ok. The man smiled and nodded but didn't move to leave and moved the handkerchief again towards her encouragingly. "No really, thank you, I'm ok, just… embarrassed."

"May I?" he asked, motioning to the empty chair across from her.

"Yes, yes, of course, although I'd best be going." Bessie's eyes flicked to her phone. She still had time but didn't want to risk being late for the appointment given the stakes. The man sat and was still, as if he had all the time in the world and he'd known her forever. She felt comfortable with him even though she never was comfortable around anyone new, especially strange men in a big city.

She didn't move to leave. Her crying had slowed but a wayward tear drizzled down her cheek which she caught with the handkerchief, smiling with resignation at her new friend. Bessie started to calm down a bit and noticed her friend was wearing a small silver badge with his name on it. "Mr. Price?" She asked. He looked a bit confused for a second and then remembered his badge, nodding slowly and smiling. Bessie extended her hand. "I'm Bessie." They shook hands.

A moment passed and then, surprising herself, Bessie just spilled out her story without edits or formality. Mr. Price was a good listener and took it in without a word, expressing his encouragement with a facial expression at the appropriate times. When she was finished, she felt better for no reason other than to have told someone about the situation and to have them care enough to listen. She glanced up at the building, and then her watch. "I guess I'd better head over there." Bessie started to pack the trash on the table, wiping it down with a napkin and gathering herself to leave.

"Bessie," Mr. Price said, "I happen to have a friend at the bank who might be able to help. Her name is Mrs. Winslow and it might be worth asking after her when you are done with your meeting."

"Oh, that's very kind of you. Thank you so much," she said with some surprise. "I'll... I'll do that."

"Please do, you will like her, she's a good friend," Mr. Price stated, "and please feel free to use my name when you call on her."

"Mr. Price, thank you so much for your kindness." Bessie motioned to the handkerchief. "Please allow me to clean this and get it back to you."

He reached into his jacket and handed her a card. "No rush at all, just stop by when you have time, or keep it if you prefer."

Bessie thanked him again and got her things together to leave, feeling oddly peaceful and even a bit confident. She stopped and said, "I really don't know what I would have done if I hadn't run into you."

He smiled warmly. "I feel fortunate to have met you, young lady, and I know things will work out just fine."

It sounded so obvious when he said it that it gave Bessie no small degree of faith that he might possibly be right.

— — —

"Good grief." Bessie took in the darkness and couldn't believe how late it was. She had been at the bank almost all day, first meeting with the gentleman in the loan-servicing department who was pleasant but not able to help much. Since the bank had already adjusted the payment once, he said that it would be difficult to get a further adjustment and that he didn't have the authority to make that decision anyway. He told Bessie that he would bring it up to the loan committee who made those kinds of decisions but couldn't make any promises. Bessie felt like at least there was a sliver of hope and decided to focus on the possibility that it would work out.

She was so drained from the meeting she almost forgot about Mrs. Winslow, only remembering after the elevator had brought her back to the lobby. Bessie looked at her watch, it was almost three-thirty and she wondered if it was even worth trying to find Mrs. Winslow, talking herself out of it a little at a time.

"Can I help you?" A uniformed security guard brought her back.

"Oh, um, yes, I'm looking for Mrs. Winslow. My friend Mr. Price said she worked here?" she blurted in surprise.

The guard nodded officiously and looked at her with a deeper level of consideration as if he had just seen her. "Yes, ma'am." He backed off a bit and turned to the side, talking into a tiny microphone affixed to his lapel that Bessie hadn't seen in short statements. He nodded twice at the responses that must have beamed back to his invisible earpiece and then smiled at Bessie in a slightly more relaxed way that was clearly not his natural state. "Please go up to the twenty-third floor and Jayne will greet you at the elevator," he said and walked Bessie to the elevator, waving a keycard and punching the appropriate floor.

"Thank you, sir," Bessie offered, feeling anxious and wondering what was in store for her.

A woman about her mom's age, wearing a grey suit and big dangling earrings was at the elevator doors as they opened. "Bessie?" she asked with a large smile on her face.

Bessie was a little startled by the suddenness of her appearance and at hearing her name. "Oh yes, I'm Bessie. Are you Mrs. Winslow?"

"No, I'm Jayne. I'll take you in to see Mrs. Winslow in a moment. Are you hungry? Thirsty?" Jayne had turned and clearly expected Bessie to fall in behind. They walked through a wide corridor rimmed with tidy glass offices and past a conference room centered by a huge walnut-topped table with steel legs. The city spilled out below them and views were incredible.

"Wow, I feel like I'm in a spaceship," Bessie said out loud.

Jayne laughed and nodded her agreement. "This place is pretty incredible, especially given that our last headquarters was so horrible. We were in an old department store building for years and when we financed this building for some long-term customers, they gave us such an amazing deal we couldn't resist."

They stopped in front of an office with a partially open

door and etched glass windows. "This is Mrs. Winslow's office," Jayne explained, tapping on the door lightly and walking in with Bessie in tow.

Mrs. Winslow bustled over to them with open arms, her many necklaces swinging wildly and multiple earrings clanging so that she sounded like a reindeer springing from a rooftop. Her mischievous eyes were the best part of her wide and open smile, instantly melting the nerves that had been gnawing at Bessie. Mrs. Winslow wrapped her in the warm embrace of her tiny little arms before Bessie even knew what was happening.

In perpetual motion, Mrs. Winslow left the office with Jayne flicking her head at Bessie to follow. Mrs. Winslow was talking the entire time, periodically looking over her shoulder as she gestured with her hands. Bessie wasn't following the conversation entirely but was pretty sure Mrs. Winslow had asked Jayne for a snack and some coffee among other things.

After settling in the conference room and a bit of small talk, Mrs. Winslow asked how she could help. Bessie shifted uncomfortably in her chair and eventually told her the whole story. She even included the part about how she felt guilty because her private college tuition had been one of the reasons they were in such a mess to begin with. As with Mr. Price, she felt better having told someone, even if the reality hadn't changed. Mrs. Winslow was a surprisingly good listener, only interrupting to ask a question or two.

When it was clear that Bessie was done, Mrs. Winslow took a slow breath and responded. "Bessie, your story is very moving, partly because it is a familiar one to me. My own father died when I was fourteen and my mother, two brothers and I struggled for many years. We had our power shut off multiple times and there were days when we didn't have enough to eat. We certainly weren't rich before my father's death, far from it, but we lived comfortably and had enough that my mom could make our modest home a lovely place. I remember those tough times even though my life now is very different."

Bessie was shocked that this successful fireplug of a woman ever had such serious financial hardship and it made her own situation feel more normal somehow.

"I will see what I can do to help you and I'm glad Mr. Price introduced us," Mrs. Winslow said, her big smile returning.

Something about this woman filled up a well of confidence inside of Bessie and she knew she could believe her. Fighting back tears, Bessie tried to thank her but couldn't quite get the words out. Mrs. Winslow had pulled her to her feet and was giving her another one of those little elfin hugs, this one a little bit longer. She pushed Bessie back so she could look at her in the eyes.

"This will get better. And then it will be up to you to be fully in charge of your future so something like money never gets in control of your life again. Do you understand me? I will help you and then you have to help yourself."

Bessie nodded vigorously. "Yes, I know what you mean. That I am now an adult and in control of my own choices. I understand how fragile the world can be and that I don't care about ever being wealthy but I want to be fully in control of my life and not vulnerable again," Bessie gushed all at once.

Mrs. Winslow nodded firmly. "Correct. Tomorrow, I'm going to approve your new payment plan. From there, it's up to you." Mrs. Winslow smiled.

"I can't thank you enough," Bessie stuttered. "You are an amazing person... You don't even know me..."

"Actually, I think I do." Mrs. Winslow's eyes twinkled.

Jayne was waiting in the doorway, appearing as if she were beamed there from another location right on cue. Bessie turned when she got to Jayne to look back at Mrs. Winslow, but somehow she had already bounded off somewhere and was gone.

Bessie stood on the now-darkened street and took a deep breath of the frigid air, feeling relaxed for the first time in many months. She hadn't been able to eat all day. Even the nice little snack of fresh fruit Jayne brought with their coffee earlier didn't look appealing, but now she was starving. She thought she had seen a Chinese restaurant around the corner and thought she'd investigate, knowing she needed to eat before she could get in the car for a couple of hours, the dark and the snow extending the pending trip home. She tucked her scarf into her coat, pulled up her gloves and set out to find some *chow mein*, figuring it wasn't much of a victory dinner but not willing to spend a penny more than she had to.

Bessie found the little restaurant after circling the block once and could smell the tasty aroma of garlic and ginger before she entered. The place was brightly lit, clean and had a stack of take-out orders with people waiting in chairs next to the register. She was greeted warmly by the kitchen staff who yelled out a greeting as they continued to work diligently behind the counter. Bessie looked at the big menu board and thought about what she wanted when she sensed someone next to her and thought she might be in the way. She absently turned to suggest the person go ahead of her and her eyes went wide in surprise. "Bertram?" she gasped out.

He had been looking at the menu himself, wanting to try something different for a change. "Holy cow." He jumped back a bit. "Bessie?? What the heck are you doing here?" They both laughed and gave each other a big hug. "I haven't seen you since…" Bertram's face darkened and he didn't finish the thought, but he didn't need to.

Bessie was nodding. "…Dad's memorial service. I know. Things have been pretty hectic for you, I hear." Bessie stayed close to Bertram's parents and they often told her of how he was getting on. "You got promoted and moved to a big skyscraper they told me," she teased.

He hung his head a little sheepishly. "You must've been talking to my mom. Yeah, I live just around the corner," he said, pointing toward the apartment building with a flick of the head. "Do you know what you want?" Bertram asked, turning to a few people who had been patiently waiting behind them.

"Oh, sorry," Bessie said to the forming queue, stepping to the counter to order. "Bertram, what's good?"

Despite his intentions to try something new, he blurted, "Let's get two orders of the garlic noodles – they're legendary."

She nodded. "That sounds perfect." They each paid for their own order and moved off to the side to wait. "Do you want to sit down and catch up? I've got a long drive and want to eat here."

Bertram really didn't have time to hang out. He had a pile of paperwork to do for the quarter end and hadn't even started it, but he found himself saying, "Yes," immediately in spite of that. He couldn't quite take his eyes off of Bessie and found that more than a little unnerving. "What is my deal?" he wondered, chastising himself for staring.

They found a table far enough from the door that they wouldn't get blasted every time someone came in to grab their take-out and took a seat. Bertram and Bessie immediately started talking and sharing little stories, as if eight years and lifetimes of experiences hadn't changed a thing. They were just Bertram and Bessie, two unlikely friends who felt familiar and comfortable catching up on their lives. Strangely, they hadn't spent much time at all together since they went away to college. With their interests differing so much and Bertram not coming back home often, there wasn't opportunity to visit and they had drifted apart. You wouldn't have guessed that by looking at them, though. In fact, they were so engrossed in conversation, the owner finally came over with their food.

"Sorry to interrupt, but this was getting cold and I know you like the noodles very hot, Mr. Bertram." He handed them their noodles, smiling and bowing slightly.

They laughed and thanked him, taking a moment to situate their food. They looked at each other as each of them slurped up their noodles at roughly the same time, sparking laughter from both of them.

Two hours later, Bertram walked Bessie to her car. "It was so great to see you... What a small world." Bessie was fishing for her keys. Bertram felt a little melancholy but he wasn't sure why. "Are you sure you don't want to come up to the apartment?" She shot him a look and rolled her eyes. "No, no, I have a second bedroom and I'm worried about you driving home in the snow." He tried to allay her concerns, knowing that it came out wrong and his not-so-virtuous reputation had probably made its way to her through his mom and his siblings.

Bessie softened. "No – thanks, though. I need to get home. I've got classes in the morning... but I did really enjoy seeing you."

Bertram resisted the urge to try to kiss her, especially since it was clear that it was not on her to-do list at that moment, finding himself chastising his impulse to lean in for the attempt even after he told himself to behave. "What the heck am I doing??" he asked himself, a little flustered.

Bessie gave him a big hug and he watched her pull the old sedan out of the parking lot, pay the automated attendant, only turning around towards home when he couldn't hear the sound of her muffler anymore. "Man," he thought, "you've got to get it together, bro'." He said the last part out loud.

Determined not to be late to dinner with Norman and Irma, Bertram slid into the firm leather seat of his BMW and sped towards the address. His GPS piped periodic instructions to him as the tall buildings of the city gave way to the low-lying suburban homes and retail shops that rimmed the area like a seawall, stretching out many miles in front of him.

About ten miles out of town he drove into Norman's neighborhood, watching his speed since he already had two tickets and the next one would be problematic, especially given his financial situation. Nothing had changed there and he was doing his best to ignore it, even though the pressure was becoming more real as each month had more days in it than dollars. He pulled up to a very nice ranch-style house in a mature neighborhood that reminded him a little of home. The homes weren't quite as old and most of them looked as if they had gotten a facelift of some kind fairly recently.

He parked the car out front and waited a moment, half-listening to a familiar song on the radio before going in. He hadn't been able to get Bessie off of his mind and he wasn't sure why. Bertram had never thought much about the women he dated, while he enjoyed their company, and he certainly wasn't used to thinking about a woman he'd never dated at all! He reached into the back seat for the bottle of wine he had brought and walked toward the front door that was painted a bright red, feeling a little anxious for no known reason. All he knew at that moment is that he was almost broke, was beginning to obsess about a woman who lived in the town he had escaped and hadn't seen in years, and was dying to taste whatever that was that filled the air with a fragrance he'd never experienced.

Irma answered the door with a huge grin wearing an apron that said, '*Rock Lobster*' and had a picture of a lobster playing an electric guitar. "Norman, Bertram is here," she tossed over her shoulder as she hugged Bertram by way of introduction, taking his coat and wine in one deft movement.

Irma was tall, at least five feet eleven, and had that same smooth way as Norman of moving in a flowing way, almost like she was dancing to some inaudible music. "Come in, come in, please make yourself welcome."

Bertram could hear voices and laughing in the kitchen but Irma pointed toward the other side of the house. "Norman is in there watching basketball – he probably can't hear me over the racket," she explained. "Just go on back. There's beer and water back there… Do you want something else?" she asked. He thanked her and said he was fine, wandering back to find Norman.

Norman and two other men were watching college basketball with the intensity of snipers, punctuating the action with cries of distress or joy depending upon the event in question. It took a moment or two before Norman noticed his friend standing there and, apologizing deeply for his rudeness, he stood, gave Bertram a big hug and introduced him to his brother-in-law, Joe, and nephew, Donald.

They both came over and shook Bertram's hand with a pleasant, "Hello!" and Donald motioned him to a spot on the couch. It felt great to Bertram just to hang out and enjoy the game, even though neither team was all that important to him. It didn't take more than a few minutes for him to feel like he'd been hanging with the three of them for years instead of a quarter or two of a basketball game.

Irma called the men to the table and even though the score

was tied and it was the fourth quarter, the TV was flicked off and they all dutifully made their way to the dining room. The spread was incredible. Freshly baked bread and corn muffins arranged on a bread plate, a huge copper serving bowl of what must've been the famous gumbo in the center of the table and multiple plates, bowls and serving dishes of vegetables, side dishes and fixings surrounding the gumbo like soldiers protecting their queen.

"Wow," was all Bertram could manage.

For the next three hours, they laughed and ate what Bertram thought must've been the best meal of his life. When he could finally not eat a single bite more he pushed back in his chair slightly, feeling a bit like a fighter who might have to throw in the towel. "Irma, that was absolutely incredible. Better than any restaurant," he said honestly. They all laughed.

"No joke," Donald agreed. "I drive all the way from Illinois on the Sundays that Mom and Irma make gumbo and would do it every weekend," he said, only half-joking. Bertram just shook his head in awe of how delicious the entire feast was.

"Well, anybody ready for dessert?"

Bertram's eyes got wide. How could anyone still eat after that? Fortunately, everyone else needed a breather too and the men headed back to the TV room after helping clear the mountain of dishes they had manufactured. Donald's wife, Margo, was clearly pregnant but was just as helpful as everyone else, shooing them out of the kitchen so they could get ready for the dessert phase a bit later. Joe and Donald were looking for the Michigan game and Norman suggested that Bertram join him for a look around the house.

They ended up in Norman's study, a small room filled with books and pictures, just around the corner from the entry foyer. There was an small antique desk with a set of built-in bookcases behind it, all stained to perfectly match the desk.

The lighting was provided by a wooden and copper floor lamp with an elaborate stained-glass shade and a desk lamp with a rough-cut redwood base and carved wooden stem. There was something both peaceful and elegant about the small room.

Norman sat down in the antique banker's chair behind the desk and motioned Bertram to sit in the armchair that was clearly designed or chosen to look like it came with the banker's chair.

Bertram looked around in admiration. "This is a beautiful room," he commented.

"Thank you very much, I'm quite fond of it too," Norman admitted.

Bertram rubbed the arms of the chair. "This looks like an antique but feels modern," he thought out loud.

Norman nodded. "Yes, I built that a few years back. Took me two tries because the first one didn't look quite right."

Bertram looked at him. "You built this?" he asked incredulously, figuring the chair cost a small fortune.

"Yes. Pretty much everything in here but the desk and that floor lamp. I've always loved working with wood and learned a lot doing all this."

Bertram surveyed the room, thinking how little he knew about most things and a bit embarrassed about how little he actually knew about his host. Thinking a bit more about it, he started to wonder how Norman could afford this kind of a place. It seemed like much more than a doorman could ever afford, even a great one like Norman.

"Norman, can I ask you something personal?" Bertram started tentatively, hoping he wouldn't offend him.

"Of course. Anything," Norman replied.

"How in the world does a doorman afford a place like this?" Bertram sputtered. Norman busted out in laughter. Bertram, feeling embarrassed, added, "I mean that's really none of my business, but…"

Norman waved off his excuses but continued to chuckle. "You want to know how a late-fifties African American guy with a seemingly menial job affords a great spread in the suburbs and duped a beauty like Irma into marrying him?" he asked, his eyes gleaming impishly.

"Basically," Bertram admitted.

"Well, that's both simple and complicated," Norman replied, looking at something on his bookshelf.

He stood up and pulled down a plaque that Bertram had noticed when he came in. It was right in the center of the bookcase and had some words engraved in neat, block letters that Bertram couldn't fully make out. Norman held it and looked at for a minute, remembering something he didn't share immediately.

"When I was about your age, I was a little bit of a knucklehead. I grew up on the wrong side of the tracks and made it worse by doing stupid things. Truth is, I was headed down a path that would've been bad news."

Bertram nodded encouragingly.

"So then as part of an extremely lucky chain of events, I got a job at a lumber supply loading wood onto trucks, mostly to fulfill large orders from builders and contractors. The gentleman who owned it, Mr. Sykes, a tough but fair man, took a liking to me for some reason and sort of treated me like the son he never had – he had three daughters. I started to get in trouble less and work more."

Norman paused a moment as if to be sure Bertram was still interested, which he clearly was.

"One day, when I was going to get my paycheck from the office, I bumped into the most beautiful girl I'd ever seen…" Norman looked out towards the kitchen and Bertram's eyes widened.

"Irma?" Bertram asked.

"Yes, that's right, it was Irma." Norman nodded. "But that's not the story. I fell madly in love with Irma. I wanted to be her man more than anything I ever wanted in my life even though I'd only seen her three times and never even talked to her for more than a greeting. Mr. Sykes, however, was not interested. He said I would have to earn the right to date his daughter and made it one hundred percent clear that there was no way I'd be able to get within twenty-five feet of her unless he stamped it with approval."

Bertram looked confused. "Dang. So how did you convince him?"

"Turns out, Mr. Sykes had something specific in mind; something he learned from his own mentor years before. He handed me this plaque and told me that until I was actually living the words engraved on it, I wouldn't even have the chance to speak with Irma, much less see if she had any interest in me."

Norman handed the plaque to Bertram. It was much older than he thought; the brass was tarnished and worn in places and the varnish on the wooden frame had been retouched many times. He handled it gingerly and read the words at the top out loud: "*The Money-Strong Creed.*" Then, with an encouraging nod from Norman, he cleared his throat and reread the heading and the five statements arranged neatly below it:

THE MONEY-STRONG CREED

Adjust your expectations

Spend less

Obey the One-Month Rule

Eliminate debt

Save the difference

He looked quizzically at Norman. "That's it? This is what Mr. Sykes asked you to do before you could get to know Irma?"

Norman nodded knowingly. "Doesn't seem like much does it? I didn't think so at first either. But then Mr. Sykes explained it and I began to see that I had a lot of work to do. Given where I started from, and who I hung with, it was like learning to speak a foreign language; one that no one I knew could understand."

Bertram wasn't sure why that was true.

Norman explained: "Mr. Sykes expected me to get to a point where I had no debt, had saved enough money that any emergency could be dealt with and to commit to living my entire life that way. The way he saw it, I might represent a chance to pass on the knowledge he had learned that had helped him to build a prosperous business but also to weather a number of big storms along the way. He wasn't willing to put Irma with anyone who didn't live their life in a way that would protect her and give her choices. Also, back in his day, it was that much more important for a person of color to have the ability to build a strong financial life since the banks and finance companies had no appetite to help you if you might need it. He wasn't going to risk Irma to someone who couldn't be financially strong."

Bertram considered this and related it to his current situation. He'd never thought about being financially strong and wasn't sure he fully understood it. It seemed like spending less and living without debt was pretty old-fashioned and didn't make sense anymore. "*Everyone has a car payment,*" he thought. Still, something about Norman made him feel totally at ease and he couldn't quite believe that Norman had a house like this one on a doorman's income.

There was a peaceful feeling inside this spacious, tastefully decorated home that reflected Norman's demeanor and

Irma's spunk and it reminded Bertram of his youth somehow; a certain simplicity that was missing from his life today. If he were being honest, going back to Weaver to visit made him almost uncomfortable. His BMW and the way he dressed looked out of place on the tree-lined driveways where older sedans and pickups were the norm.

Norman was watching Bertram's face as he reread the 'Money-Strong Creed' but he kept silent. Bertram, still digesting his thoughts, considered his words carefully.

"I can see how this would have helped you, since, well, you—"

"—didn't have squat?" Norman interjected with a chuckle.

Bertram looked relieved. "Well yeah," he paused. "I mean for someone like me, I've already got some debt and a car payment and make a great income. I'm living the way I should be living, the way I'm expected to." Bertram seemed to be sorting his thoughts out as he spoke.

Norman just nodded. "You're right. It's expected that you have a nice car, a fancy apartment, and all the right stuff in it, when you work a professional job. Plus, lots of people your age love to go out to eat and have excellent taste in restaurants. It wasn't any different when I was coming up. That was what Mr. Sykes wanted to protect Irma from. He grew up after the Depression and money was always tight. He told me a story about how he almost lost his business once because he had expanded too quickly and got stuck in a housing recession in the seventies. Mr. Sykes told me he went from dialing up suppliers to try to give the builders what they had ordered, to begging banks to not repossess his trucks and equipment, and to loan him enough money to survive once the orders dried up. He barely survived. During that time he met someone who helped him learn the *Creed* – another business owner who took him under his wing. It wasn't easy but he got himself completely out of debt and to the point where the business had a cash cushion. Over time, he always had one year of expenses saved to be sure he could weather another mishap." Norman paused.

Bertram couldn't help but flash back to the conversation he'd had with Bessie and how not having enough savings and the burden of her family's mortgage was putting her in a very similar spot now that the factory had run into issues.

Donald popped his head in. "Gentlemen, Irma has served the dessert and requests your presence."

Norman chuckled. "Thanks, Donald. Better not let those pies sit there alone." He moved to stand up.

"Oh," Donald said impishly to Bertram, "you're getting indoctrinated." Bertram nodded and smiled.

"I'm not sure Bertram's quite ready for this one yet," Norman said. "Remember how long it took your sorry butt to catch on?" He gave Donald a little shake by the shoulders and a wide grin as he loped past, calling on them to follow.

Irma had two pies majestically sitting in the middle of the table, one pecan and the other cherry. Bertram had never seen more perfect pie crust and even though he was still stuffed from dinner, he couldn't help having a nice-size slice of both. "Irma, I'm moving in," is all he could manage to say when he'd taken his very last bite. They all laughed.

"Norman and Irma's kids almost never left for the same reason," Joe piped. "I think their daughter, Lottie, tried to convince her husband to live with her parents for the first three years of their marriage."

Norman shook his head slowly with a wide grin. "So true."

Bertram's drive back to the city gave him some time with his thoughts. The *'Money-Strong Creed'* was swirling around in his head, especially the casual conversation he'd had with Donald after dessert. Donald had told him about his own difficult situation after college where he had racked up a bunch of student-loan debts. Then, when he got out of school, he went to work for a start-up that paid well but got shut down after about two years, just long enough for him to pile on some credit-card debt and buy a townhouse. When he lost his job, he didn't have much at all in savings, figuring the stock he'd been granted when he came to work would be his 'nest egg'. Now with that basically worthless, no income, plenty of obligations and a serious girlfriend, he had to get real.

With Norman's help, Donald began to follow the *'Money-Strong Creed'*. He sold his townhouse, moved into a studio apartment and used the modest equity he'd built to pay off his debts, except a small portion of the student-loan burden. He worked at UPS over the holiday to earn some money and put every extra penny in savings, chipping away at the last bit of student-loan debt as well. He even asked Irma to teach him to cook a few things so he didn't have to go out to eat as much. Before he knew it, he was completely out of debt. Donald had even saved some money, allowing him to take a job that he had always wanted rather than going for the income alone. He was happily expecting their first child and figured he'd be able to buy a small house in a year or so with a large down payment and some money left in the bank for emergencies. Donald was *Money-Strong*.

Bertram wasn't sure. He'd worked very hard to achieve the lifestyle he was living and didn't want to step backwards. His friends were all professionals and they seemed to be able to make it work pretty easily so he couldn't see how he was any different or why he would want to be. He loved the convenience of his building and the fact that his many friends could crash in the guest room after epic parties or just whenever they were in town visiting. He acknowledged that he didn't 'need' the BMW, but felt he deserved it; a reward for all of his daily efforts and his recent promotion. In fact, there was nothing he would change about his lifestyle at all, he thought indignantly. He slumped against his seat as he stopped at the light at the bottom of his exit.

"That's all true," he said out loud, "but... Bessie?" He wasn't even sure what that meant, or why he said it, but Bertram did know that he hadn't been able to get her out of his head since seeing her, and that it was adding to his agitation.

He swung into the garage and parked in his designated spot, turning off the car and sitting there in the dark. "*What if?*" he thought. Then he shook it off and got out of the car, heading to the elevator bay for the ride up to his apartment.

Bessie was feeling thankful and sad at the same time. She was thankful for Mr. Price and Mrs. Winslow. She had heard from the bank that the loan committee had approved their request to further reduce their payment and had even given them two years with the new payment structure before it would go back to the normal amount. This would be enough to get her through the credential program and even to the place when she was receiving full teaching wages after her student teaching was complete. With her mom's part-time hours and her café money, they could get by every month and survive. But Bessie still wasn't sure it was enough. They'd been through so much lately and the truth was, they were only one small problem away from being in trouble again financially. With no savings and no extra money to speak of at the end of each month, all it would take was her mom to lose her hours or for the café to slow down during the summer and they would be right back where they were before. She thought a lot about it and decided that they should list the house for sale at the end of the spring, giving them the ability to pay off the mortgage and buy a small place for her mom. She could find an apartment somewhere close to the elementary school, maybe even in between the school and her mother's new place.

It wasn't what she wanted. Bessie had so many memories and had lived all but four years of her life under the same roof and her father's kind, generous energy still seeped out of every rafter. Not just that, her mom's art studio would be hard to replicate – something she'd spent many years building and many hours pouring her creative energy into would be gone. Bessie's heart ached over the decision, yet she knew it was the right one.

She had been scared to share the thought with her mom, figuring that after all the effort she would have to cajole her into it over time. But when Bessie finally worked up the courage and told her mom over dinner one Saturday, she just nodded and said, "Makes a lot of sense," before taking a sip of her wine and commenting on how the cherry trees around the town square were blooming early that year. Bessie was both relieved and a little at odds, almost hoping to be talked out of the decision.

While they were putting away the dishes, Bessie's mom sat

against the counter, drying her hands with a kitchen towel and watching her daughter. Bessie noticed this and stopped, looking at her mom.

"I'm so proud of you, Bessie," her mom said simply, looking at her daughter with a serene smile. Bessie, not prone to overt displays of emotion, immediately began to cry and the two women hugged each other, holding each other close enough that the world couldn't pry its way in.

Bertram pushed back from his desk and rubbed his eyes. One quarter down and nowhere near the growth targets that Mr. Vaughan had set. He knew it would be tough to achieve; his territory didn't have a lot of new businesses moving in and out and their competitors were well-established. He'd worked harder than ever, driving his team as well, and he was still only was able to rack up twenty percent more business than the first quarter in the prior year. While this improvement was respectable, it was barely more than half what Bertram needed. If he was going to hit the numbers, something would have to be different, but he had no idea what that might be.

Other areas of Bertram's life were also taking unusual turns and he felt a little like he was walking on the bow of a bobbing ship, blindfolded. Many of the things he thought he aspired to – a luxury apartment, a high-end ride, multiple girlfriends and a freewheeling lifestyle – weren't all bringing him the joy he'd expected.

Since his dinner at Norman and Irma's, he'd been thinking a lot about the '*Money-Strong Creed*', still unable to wrap his brain around how it was possible to start adopting any of it when there was no extra money to begin with. He and Norman saw each other frequently but Bertram kept their conversation light and didn't linger around to shoot the breeze like he'd often done before. Norman gave him the space to do his own thing while being as friendly and helpful as ever.

Meanwhile, Bertram had been in touch with Bessie, despite resisting the urge to contact her. He finally admitted to himself that he might have some feelings toward her, a fact that was surprising to him since they had almost nothing other than some of their history in common. Moreover, he was very experienced in not having feelings for any woman he'd ever dated, making it a well-developed practice not to get too close. Besides, he didn't see how a serious girlfriend fit his image or his schedule. In his playbook, he never reached out to someone after a date, much less go on more than a few with the same person. That said, things were shifting, despite his resistance. Although he didn't really consider the chance meeting at the Chinese restaurant an official date, and wasn't even sure if Bessie felt anything at all for him, he had texted her soon after. He pretended like he wanted to be sure she'd gotten back safely, but really saw it as an excuse to keep in touch.

He remembered with some embarrassment calling his friend, Simon, "Emo" whenever he'd be smiling while texting back and forth with his girlfriend. Simon always took it in his low-key, good-natured way but Bertram felt a little like a hypocrite looking back on it, since almost every text Bessie sent him made him grin. If nothing else, connecting with Bessie was a welcome break from the other stresses in his life, even if it was a little unsettling as well.

Bertram was looking out the window of his office when his email notification chimed. It wasn't good news. His second-largest account, NetCore, one that he'd brought in during his first year at the company, was giving them written notice that they were moving to a competitor. Bertram's heart almost stopped. Without NetCore, not only would his territory results be in the toilet overnight but his personal commission would drop by about twenty percent. This meant that his monthly pay would be about the same as before the promotion.

He should have taken a couple of deep breaths to settle his nerves but instead he immediately called Dave Grossman, his contact at NetCore. Dave didn't answer so he left a voice mail, an unpleasant one that he regretted as soon as he hung up. He knew it wasn't Dave's fault but he was floored that he wouldn't have given him any notice – he'd taken Dave to two NFL games and a couple of NBA games, not to mention lots of expensive dinners over the years. How could Dave have done this to him? Bertram was sitting and steaming when Vaughan walked in.

"What happened with NetCore?" Vaughan demanded. "You've had that account for years."

Bertram could only shake his head. "I don't know," he seethed, just wanting Vaughan to let him take his defeat alone.

"Well, you better figure it out. There's no way you'll hit your year-end target without them unless you can replace them within the month." Vaughan seemed to be rubbing it in. "Let me know what your plan is next week," Vaughan added as he walked out.

Bertram sat very still for about two minutes. Then he picked up his desk phone and threw it against the wall where it shattered into about fifty pieces. He grabbed his jacket and stormed out.

Bertram had walked to the office that morning and he powered down the street towards his apartment. He took a detour through the park and felt his blood recede from a boil to a simmer, then found a bench in front of a statue he'd never really noticed where he took a seat and tried to collect himself. He was feeling more than a little sorry for himself and wasn't sure what to do next. His phone rang. It was in his jacket pocket so he had to fish around for it where it lay in a crumpled ball next to him. "Hello?"

"Bertram?" the light, even voice on the other end asked.

"Bessie…" He felt his body relax almost instantly. "How are you?"

"I'm good thanks… How are you?" Bessie replied.

Bertram thought for a second. "I'm great too, thanks," he fibbed. "What are you up to?" He thought keeping things focused on her would help him avoid talking about his situation.

"Well, I'm calling because we were just getting the house ready for sale and I happened to find a few of your things," she said. "A letterman jacket that you must've loaned me at some point and I never returned, plus a few odds and ends. I could just give them to your mom and dad if you'd like or put them in the yard sale… Thought I'd ask which you'd prefer."

"Oh, thanks, you can just put them in the yard sale. Man, I can't believe you're actually moving. Are you doing ok?" He wasn't usually good at this kind of conversation, preferring not to talk about things that might be uncomfortable but secretly hoping that she'd called because she needed his support.

"Yes, actually, I'm ok," she answered. "I think I've had enough time to sort through the whole thing so that now that it's actually happening, it's not too bad."

"Ok, that's good, really good to hear." Bertram didn't want the conversation to end. "Have you found a new place yet?" he asked, partially to prolong the conversation.

"No, not yet. Figure we've got a bit before the house sells and it's probably too early to start looking seriously. Mrs. Benson did mention that her tenant in the carriage house was leaving and that she'd be happy to rent it to me. It's kind of perfect since I'll be teaching at Anderson. I could walk when the weather is good. We'll see if the timing works."

Mrs. Benson had been their fifth-grade teacher at Anderson when they were kids and she and her husband lived in one of the larger older homes just off the square. The carriage house was above the garage and was tiny but Bertram could see why it might appeal to Bessie. "That could be really great," he offered.

"Excuse me." Bessie was giving someone instructions about moving a piece of furniture or something. "Hey, Bertram, I've got to run. Mom is looking for me to help decide what should stay and what is going to be moved down for the garage sale," she explained.

"Oh, no problem, ok." Bertram paused for a moment. "Hey Bessie," Bertram started. "I… well… would you want to have dinner with me next week? I'm going to come by and visit my parents next Saturday." He winced and held his breath, waiting for another rejection to cap off his day.

She was quiet for a second. "Sure, that would be nice. Come by at six and we'll wander into town."

Bertram did a little fist pump. "Ok, that's great. See you soon, hope the sale goes well this weekend." And just like that, the day got a little bit better.

"Hey, Norman!" Bertram waved as he entered the lobby.

"Hi, Bertram, how was the day?" Norman asked. "You're home awful early for a weekday – I'm not used to seeing you back before dinner time."

Bertram sighed. "Yeah, I cut out a little early and took a walk through the park," he replied, leaving out the temper tantrum and his call with Bessie. Bertram pushed the elevator button but when it came he let the doors close.

"Everything ok, Bertram?" Norman asked, concerned.

Bertram walked over to Norman's desk. "Honestly? Not really. Things are going badly at work on a number of fronts and the truth is, I'm struggling a little financially. I didn't want to share this with you before because, well, I'm not sure why." Bertram looked at Norman to see if he was judging him but Norman only looked worried about his friend and waited for him to continue.

"I've hit a... rough patch. My income is down and I can't really afford the way I'm living. I'm also too embarrassed to tell any of my friends or my family so I feel like an idiot and isolated at the same time. Plus I'm not sure how to fix it – nothing I can think of will put it all back to the way it was before. It feels pretty hopeless." Bertram was happy to have let it all out but was worried that his friend would think less of him.

Norman just nodded. "Lots of people are in the same place you are – I see it every day. The circumstances might be different, but the issues are the same. When you don't have a safety net, life can easily get the best of you sometimes."

Bertram nodded. "I've been thinking a lot about the creed, you know, the '*Money-Strong Creed*'. I just don't see how it applies once you're already in a position like mine. I mean once you've already got yourself in a lifestyle and a fair amount of debt, it seems like it's too late, right? I mean you were able to implement the *Creed* before you had too much baggage. I already have the baggage – how could I implement it now?"

Norman thought for a moment. "You know, in some ways, the '*Money-Strong Creed*' is actually *more* important later on because it's the only way you regain your freedom from your choices and your reality. Lots of people have money problems because they can't change their expectations and constantly make bad financial decisions. Once they've gained some status, they can't figure out how to justify going backwards. Everyone strives for the next thing: the bigger house, the flashier car, a business card with a fancy title. These are all based upon the expectations we have and how we want other people to see us. No one wants to go backwards... How do you explain it to yourself or to your friends? That way of thinking," Norman pointed to his head, "it's a trap. One that's self-created, but it's still real."

Bertram's mind flashed to Bessie and how it seemed like she was perfectly fine living with her mom or in a small carriage house.

Norman went on, "The most difficult thing in the world is recognizing that you have to lower your standards, especially once the world has proven that you can have things you want even if you can't really afford them."

Bertram thought about that for a moment. "So what you're saying is that I have to expect less out of myself so I'm not disappointed in the results? Seems like a cop-out..."

Norman considered Bertram's words. "No. What I'm saying is that you have to find a way to lower your standards of what an acceptable apartment, or car, or special dinner is and find other things to appreciate that are in line with being financially fit. Just like when you were training for football season and you limited your life to the things that would help you be a great player. Your expectations wouldn't allow you to go out partying all night during the season or to eat garbage food. This is the same thing you can do in your personal life and it's the key to getting *Money-Strong*. If you are expecting filet mignon and you get a fish stick you might be disappointed but if you are expecting a fish stick and get a fish stick, all is well in the world."

"Like if you were expecting gumbo and Irma served Chef Boyardee instead?" Bertram joked.

Norman laughed hard and slapped his knee. "Exactly. Exactly. Now you're getting it – that would be a disappointing day indeed!"

Bertram sat quietly as Norman greeted some of the residents who were streaming in after their workday, nodding at the people he knew. "I think I understand what you mean. If I adjust my expectations to a lower standard, I won't make bad financial decisions. But I still don't know how that will help me out of my current situation."

Norman nodded understandingly. "Think about it this way: if you changed where you thought you *should* be living and just looked at what you could afford, would you still live in your apartment?"

Bertram stared at Norman. "Well... I guess not. I mean I don't know how I'd throw the epic parties everyone's gotten used to without a pad like that."

Norman cut him off. "Right so you *expect* to live in a place where you can do that but could you still throw an awesome party at a pub or somewhere you didn't live?"

Bertram considered the idea. "Yes, I guess that's possible. I know that one of the guys that lives in a studio on the sixth floor periodically has his friends hang out with him at O'Grady's around the corner to watch his favorite hockey team."

Norman was nodding. "Yep, now you get it. Once your expectations change, your options expand, even though you are making smarter financial decisions. You actually have *more* options not fewer, when you have lower expectations. If you're dead-set on something specific, your options are limited."

Bertram felt like he was beginning to understand what Norman was saying but he also felt overwhelmed.

As if he were reading Bertram's mind, Norman smiled and pulled him in for a hug. "Don't hurt your brain on this stuff too much. Just chew on it... You know where to find me." Norman released him and looked him straight in the eye. "Doing this kind of work on your financial situation is courageous. And it's hard. Don't be too hard on yourself, I'll help in any way I can."

"Thanks, Norman, you've given me a lot to think about." Bertram wandered back to the elevator bay. "Plus all this talk of filet mignon and gumbo has made me hungry," he joked.

"Don't forget the fish sticks," Norman chided.

Back at the office the following day, Bertram felt sheepish about his behavior. He went out of his way to say hello to everyone who was there already and made his way back to his office, passing Mr. Vaughan's darkened office en route. He knew he needed to say something to Vaughan, especially since he suspected that his little spasm was already well-known around the office, but wasn't really sure what exactly to share and how to explain his behavior.

Bertram didn't have any kind of relationship with his boss and he wasn't used to that. All of his previous bosses had been mentors and the kind of work-based friendships that made you look forward to your job and even a little more motivated to succeed. There was none of that with Vaughan. He had no idea whether Mr. Vaughan valued him or his work, and he didn't know anything at all about Vaughan personally.

Bertram was so distracted thinking about how he was going to approach Vaughan that it didn't immediately register that his office phone was no longer spread across the floor like an upended jigsaw puzzle. Once he discovered that, he noticed that a nice new phone sat in the appropriate spot on his desk and that a message light was flashing. Pleased that all was magically back to normal, Bertram shook his head at his own behavior. "Hothead," he said out loud.

He picked up the receiver to listen to his voicemail but even before he pushed the button, his heart sank.

"*Oh crap, it's Dave Grossman,*" he thought, remembering his message. He winced as he pushed the little play icon and steadied himself for what was coming.

"Hey Bertram, it's Dave Grossman. I just wanted to give you a call... I left my position at NetCore last Friday and honestly, I'm not sure what they're going to do with your account. Among other things, I heard that they were considering buying one of your competitors which would mean that you guys would be cut off. Anyway, sorry for not getting to you sooner, I've been busy getting set up in my new venture. Feel free to call me at 463-785-1616. This is my new mobile number, the last phone belonged to NetCore. Ok, bye for now, hope to hear from you."

Bertram paused for a moment before looking up at the ceiling. He wasn't a religious man but this was almost too good to be true. He felt enormous relief that Dave didn't get his voicemail yesterday and he couldn't believe how stupid he had been to not give Dave the benefit of the doubt. Bertram was eager to call Dave and see what he was up to and resolved to keep in touch with him... He'd always liked him and found that Dave was one of those clients he actually enjoyed hanging out with.

While he was listening to Dave's voicemail, he saw Mr. Vaughan arrive and head to his office. Bertram took a deep breath and collected his thoughts. He still wasn't sure how to approach his boss so he called Dave's new number to buy a little time.

"Hey, Bertram, how's it going?" Dave answered.

"It's great, Dave, thanks for asking. How are you?" Bertram

responded.

"Doing great, doing great. Excited to be on to my next adventure…" Dave's voice sounded like he'd won the lottery, making Bertram laugh.

"Well, by the sound of your voice, you must be on to something really amazing. What are you up to?"

"Yes, for sure. Something I've been wanting to do for a while but just couldn't push myself over the edge. I'm going to be a full-time photographer!" Dave exclaimed, like he was announcing that he'd won a Rhodes scholarship.

Bertram's face crinkled with confusion. "Man, that's great," he offered, not sure what else to say.

"I know, I know, you think I'm crazy, so let me explain. Over the past five years, I've gotten really into photography – taking classes, working a few side projects and donating some time to take pictures for some special events at the kids' school. I really love it and I figure I can get by and do something I truly enjoy. It's a little scary but mostly just exciting." Dave practically spurted the words out.

Bertram took a seat. "Wow, man, that's great. What a big change… I mean, don't you have one kid headed to college and the other headed there soon? Are you sure you'll be ok?" Bertram felt like he was prying a bit but was genuinely concerned as well.

"Yes, Marissa is a sophomore this year and Justin will be going into college next year. We can't afford to send them to a fancy private school, but we talked about it before the college hunt got serious and they didn't want to anyway. I've been preparing for this so it's really no big deal. Obviously, I will still have to earn some money, but not very much. My wife, Myrna, is working so that helps as well."

Bertram felt there must be more to the story. Dave had a pretty serious job and a large salary. He'd had kids when he was young and was probably only fifteen years older than Bertram. Myrna was an administrative assistant at a commercial plumbing company which was a great job that she enjoyed, but she wasn't a big earner. How could he step away from it? "Dave, that's great. I mean it's kind of amazing that you can pull it off," Bertram said with genuine reverence.

"Thanks, Bertram. I must admit, it wasn't easy. About eight years ago I realized I wasn't having much fun at work anymore. The problem was, I didn't know what I wanted to do, I just knew the various ideas I was drawn to weren't likely to earn anywhere close to what I was making. Worse than that, I had no options – we had a big house and a big mortgage, two newer cars with payments and a bunch of debt from things we couldn't live without. It was a mess. Myrna and I had a friend who had gotten their financial situation completely in order and he told us how to do the same. The first thing he pointed out was that we had to sell the house and downsize."

"That must have been a tough pill to swallow," Bertram offered, fascinated.

"Yes, it was super-hard. The kids didn't understand the decision, especially when they saw their rooms at the new house we moved into – they were literally half the size. It was still close enough that they could stay in the same school and ride bikes to their friends' houses and honestly, it kind of brought our family a little closer together."

"Probably literally!" Bertram joked.

Dave laughed. "For sure. From there, we sold our cars and got into decent, but frankly pretty ugly, used ones. Why do you think I always made you drive us to the games? The money we saved helped us pay down the rest of our debt pretty quickly and then we just took the amount we used to use to cover our debt payments and saved that amount once the debt was totally paid off. Now, we have solid savings and low expenses so I can do what I want, instead of what I must. It's a great feeling." Dave was obviously proud of the accomplishment. As if reading Bertram's mind he added, "Getting past my own ego was the hard part. The rest was easy."

Bertram finished the conversation with Dave, promising to stay in touch and hung up the phone. *"Dave is either crazy, or courageous – I'm really not sure which,"* Bertram thought.

He couldn't help but wonder if maybe Norman was right. If he just downsized his apartment, he could solve his money problems almost immediately. He'd still have the debt and a big car payment, but he wouldn't be right on the edge of not making his minimum payments every month. With NetCore's commission now vaporized, he really didn't see that he had a choice, which in some ways made the whole thing easier. Thinking about how much bigger Dave's decision was to uproot his family, sell his house and both of his cars, it made him feel a little ashamed that he was still holding onto his lifestyle so tightly.

His eyes flicked to his phone and he realized the morning was half gone. *"Time to suck it up and talk to Vaughan,"* he thought, still not sure what he was going to say.

Bertram knocked twice on Mr. Vaughan's open door.

"Mmm," Vaughan replied without looking up from his computer screen.

"Got a moment?" Bertram asked.

Vaughan finished typing a line or two and motioned to a seat with his thumb, reading over what he had written. He turned toward Bertram. "What can I do for you?" He sounded somewhere between bored and irritated.

"Well," Bertram started, "I wanted to apologize."

Vaughan's eyes went up, showing a rare moment of facial emotion. "For what, exactly?" he asked.

"More than one thing, I guess. I'm sorry about how I handled the annual bonus conversation. You were right that I didn't read it properly and that wasn't your fault. Also, when

I got the news about NetCore, I was surprised by it and I shouldn't have been. It's my job to know what's happening in my accounts and that was on me."

Vaughan nodded and waited to see if Bertram was finished.

"I guess the final thing is, I broke my phone yesterday and that was stupid… I shouldn't have taken my frustration out that way." Bertram shook his head, obviously embarrassed about the incident. Vaughan didn't reply immediately so Bertram figured that he was done and stood to leave.

"Bertram, please have a seat," Vaughan asked, taking off his readers and rubbing the bridge of his nose. "I appreciate your apology. Frankly, I haven't known whether you had it in you to have an honest conversation and I'm glad you've done that. You have a ton of potential but you spend too much time trying to *look* good when all you have to do is just *be* good." Vaughan looked to see if Bertram understood. "I don't know much about football," Vaughan continued, "but I understand you were quite a player in college?"

Bertram was surprised he knew this; he'd never discussed his football career with Vaughan. "Well, I did my best," he replied honestly.

"I'm curious – when you did your best, did you get good results for the team?" Vaughan asked. "Not always, but most of the time, yes. When I tried as hard as I could, good things happened," Bertram acknowledged.

Vaughan nodded. "If you approach your job here the same way, good things will happen here too. Focus on what you can contribute every day. Do your best. Don't worry about the pay – it's like the scoreboard and you need to run good plays to score. Just do good work, the rest will work itself out." And with that, something astonishing happened – Vaughan flashed him a full-faced, open smile.

Bertram smiled back. "You might know something about football after all," he suggested. They shook hands and

Bertram went back to his office, firmly resolved to put his all into his job and feeling positive for the first time in quite a while.

Bertram made an effort to get back to the apartment building in time to talk to Norman before he went home for the day. He wanted to share a decision, one that had been a tough to make but that Norman would likely understand – he was going to move to a smaller place, hopefully as soon as he could.

Norman was chatting with another tenant, one Bertram didn't recognize, so he hung back until they'd finished. The tenant seemed to be sharing something emotional and Norman was listening intently, as was his way. Bertram occupied himself texting back and forth a little with Simon and then sent a note to Bessie about the weekend. When he looked up, Norman was towering over him, sending a shadow that got his attention. "Dude, you're scary quiet for a big man!"

Norman laughed and gave him a hand up, ending in a quick hug. "Good to see you, Bertram. Two days in a row, my goodness!"

"Thanks Norman, me too… Do you have a minute or two? I was hoping I would catch you before you left for the day," Bertram asked.

"Of course, of course," Norman said immediately. They wandered over to a leather bench over by Norman's glass standup desk and sat down together. "What's on your mind, Bertram?" Norman sat back against the wall and visibly relaxed.

"You're on your feet a lot, I guess," Bertram said, never really thinking about how hard it must be to stand up all day.

"Yeah, but I like it," Norman said. "I get some good exercise for sure." He smiled at Bertram warmly.

Bertram fidgeted slightly in his seat, not sure how to start. "Norman, you know how we were talking about the '*Money-Strong Creed*' and I didn't really understand what it meant to 'adjust my expectations'?" Norman nodded encouragingly but stayed quiet. "I… I think I need to do that. I mean, I know I need to do that."

Norman waited patiently for Bertram to continue.

"I've always thought that having things that made me look successful was important. I wanted people to see that I was doing well and frankly, maybe even wanted their envy a little, if I'm honest. I'm super-competitive and that's probably just one more way that I compete with others. Plus, my legendary parties have become a part of how my friends see me, what they've come to expect from me. So my apartment has been really important and I love to show it off. Unfortunately, I simply can't afford it. I've been thinking about this for days and there's no way I can afford to stay in it." Bertram looked defeated and was staring at some random spot on the floor instead of at Norman.

"I'd say that's good news!" Norman exclaimed. "Good work, Bertram!!" He clapped Bertram on the back.

Bertram looked at him like he thought maybe Norman was making fun of him, but could see that he was being genuine. Norman's face was relaxed in that reassuring smile he sometimes wore. "How's that?" Bertram shot back, irritated. "It's 'good work' that I can't afford my apartment??"

Norman looked amused. "No, that's not the good-news part. I'm sorry you don't feel like you can afford it and I know it means a lot to you. What's good news is that you have just taken your first step towards getting yourself financially fit. You've adjusted your expectations about your housing situation," Norman explained. "That's a big deal."

Bertram softened. "Thanks, I guess. Yeah, it's weird that going to a smaller place also feels like a win somehow if you're following the *Creed*. Now I have to figure out how to break my lease and find something I can afford quickly enough that I don't destroy my credit by not paying rent. Not quite sure where to start."

Norman thought for a moment. "Do you know Doug Sutter, on the sixth floor? I think he's a big sports nut like you…" Bertram shook his head. "Doug's a good guy… Went through a tough divorce not that long ago. Now he is trying to move out of his studio… He's getting custody of his kids and he is in the process of trying to get a bigger place. Not sure if he needs one as swanky as yours…" Norman shrugged and trailed off.

"Man, that could be perfect. We could just swap? Wow." Bertram tried not to get excited; it seemed too good to be true.

"Well, why don't I call up there and if he's there, you two can chat about it?" Norman suggested.

"Awesome, please do… I'll even pop over there today if he's around."

Norman walked to his desk and rang Doug's number, had a quick conversation, and beckoned Bertram over. He scribbled something onto a lined notepad, tore off the page and handed it to Bertram. "He's there but about to head out," Norman explained. "Here's his apartment number and his mobile. Why don't you give him a call? Maybe you can chat while he's on the road." Bertram thanked Norman profusely and turned to go.

"Hey Bertram," Norman called after him. Bertram stopped and came back toward the desk. "I'm really proud of you for taking this step. I know it can't be easy," he said.

"Thanks, Norman. It wasn't. I don't think I had too many choices if I'm honest about it."

Norman shrugged. "You always have choices. Only some of them are good ones, though." Norman flashed a smile that lit the room. Bertram laughed and said goodbye.

"Hi, this is Doug." Doug answered his phone after a couple of rings.

"Oh, hey, Doug, this is Bertram. I think Norman may have mentioned me to you? I'm calling about your apartment."

There was a brief silence while Doug registered. "Sure, sure, I remember. Hey, Bertram, how's it going?" Doug's voice was friendly and relaxed.

"Really good thanks. Is this a good time for you?"

"Yep, I just walked in the door," Doug replied, the sound of a door closing and other things happening in the background almost drowning him out. "Sorry I missed you the other day, I was heading out to pick up my kids and spent the rest of the night trying to help my son figure out his math homework. I was never good at math to begin with…"

"I'm still not good at math," Bertram joked. "It's probably partially why I'm trying to swap apartments…" They both laughed.

"You want to pop down and see the place?" Doug offered. "It's a little messy but you'll get the drift."

"Absolutely, I'll head down now if that works?" Bertram responded, eager to get the exchange underway. They signed off and a few moments later, Bertram was standing in Doug's kitchen.

Bertram wasn't really sure how to process Doug's apartment. It basically consisted of a tiny kitchen with an extra-skinny refrigerator; a tiled breakfast nook which wasn't really big enough for even a small table with more than two chairs; and a living area that wasn't horrible, but was lined with windows that looked directly at the building next door and had very little natural light. It took Bertram a moment to realize why there wasn't any furniture against the far wall in the living area and to digest that the wall was actually a trundle bed, forcing him recalculate the size of the living area since it also served as the bedroom. The bathroom had a shower, but no tub, and wasn't even as large as the powder room in his current place. He figured the whole apartment could fit into his current master bedroom with a little room to spare.

He didn't want to show his disappointment so he was enthusiastic and talked about a few of the details. Bertram offered to take Doug up to his place for him to get a feel for it but Doug mentioned he had already seen it.

"When were you there?" Bertram asked, a little confused. "Did you come to the Super Bowl party?" He was hoping that he didn't have to apologize for the debauchery that had ensued and genuinely had no idea if Doug had been there.

Doug laughed. "No, although I heard it was legendary. When I first moved in, I looked at it but it was too much for me. I had been through a divorce and didn't want the added stress of taking care of a large place or the extra financial obligation. The kids are young and don't mind the close quarters here. I didn't think it mattered since I just had them every other weekend. Now, since they're coming to stay full-time, a larger place seems more necessary – to keep my sanity if nothing else." Bertram chuckled. "I've given it some thought, though, and I want something less expensive, so I'm happy to have you take over my studio if you'd like, but I'm not going to be able to swap with you."

"Oh," Bertram said, unable to hide his disappointment. He was hoping this could be a smooth and easy way out of his mess, but obviously not. "Ok, well thanks for letting me know. I definitely want the studio, I've just got to figure out how to navigate getting out of this lease."

"What's your timing?" Doug asked, nodding.

"Well, as soon as I can do it, assuming I can figure out the lease issue." Bertram stopped for a minute, deciding what to share. "The truth is, I can't afford to carry my existing place, much less both of them," he blurted.

"Understand completely," Doug acknowledged, putting Bertram at ease. "No rush, just give me a couple of weeks' notice and I can move out. I already have my new place picked out and there's no time-stress on my end." Bertram shook Doug's hand, promising he'd get back to him within a week.

Bertram hoped that Norman might arrive a little early as he sometimes did on Fridays. He wasn't really sure what to do about his apartment situation and thought he might get Norman's advice. The night before, he'd been surfing through some social-media posts and saw that one of his college friends had just bought a big new house in North Carolina and couldn't help but feel envious.

Bertram tried to stay off social media, rarely posting anything, but he'd found himself drawn to it lately. This proved to be a mistake, especially since he was still feeling a little bruised by his financial predicament and every other person he knew was apparently making rock-star money and living like a head of state, or at least that's how it felt.

When he got to the lobby, Norman looked settled-in enough that he had probably been there a while, and as usual, he was joking with a couple who looked like they had just returned from a run. Bertram smiled at them as they walked toward the elevator and waved a good morning to Norman. "Hi, Bertram," he said in his smooth baritone, upbeat as always. "How's the day so far?"

Bertram couldn't help but smile himself, despite the stress and anxiety he had been totally absorbed in about his financial situation. "Pretty good, all things considered. Say,

Norman, I could use your advice on something. Do you have a minute to chat?" Bertram knew that mornings were especially busy in the lobby and didn't want to intrude.

"Of course," Norman replied immediately. "If we get interrupted, we can continue it later."

Bertram was relieved. "I went to see Doug's place – thanks for setting that up. It's not ideal but it will save me almost one thousand, three hundred dollars a month, which will make all the difference in the world. The thing is, if I can't get out of the lease on my place, it doesn't make any difference. The truth is, I'm running on fumes, moneywise. Doug wants to move and is willing to give me the studio, but he doesn't want my apartment and has something else lined up. I'm not really sure what to do."

Norman considered Bertram's situation and nodded a "good morning" to various tenants as they steadily flowed through the lobby, most of them on their way to an office somewhere. "How serious are you about your commitment to the *Money-Strong Creed*?" Norman asked after a few moments.

"You mean, overall? Or just the first step where you *'adjust your expectations'*? I… I'm totally committed. I still am trying to understand it all, but I think I'm getting the hang of it," Bertram said, somewhat unconvincingly.

Norman nodded. "Well, then I think I have an opportunity for you to achieve both of the first two *Creed* mandates in one fell swoop. You could *'adjust your expectations'* and *'spend less'* at the same time, which will get you through until you can figure out how to find a tenant for your place – assuming Doug isn't in a hurry."

Bertram looked at Norman in confusion. "How does that figure?"

Norman's eyes twinkled. "Well, my niece, Donald's older sister, is the General Manager at Downtown Kia. If you went down there with your—"

"—you want me to trade my BMW for a Kia??" Bertram jumped in, clearly thinking Norman had lost his mind. "Why would I do that? It wouldn't even save me much money... I leased the BMW and my payment isn't much more than a payment on a Kia would be."

Norman absorbed what he'd said with a look of compassion that Bertram found a little unsettling. "Yes, that may be true. No, what I was going to suggest is to see if Sylvia can help you find something used that will allow you to cut your payment in half and shorten the term of your loan. This could free up another few hundred dollars, potentially. Plus, it would have an immediate impact and help you to buy a little time to figure out your apartment situation."

Bertram listened politely and thanked Norman for the idea, taking his niece's business card and wishing him a good weekend before stepping out into the beautiful spring morning. Inside his head, however, he had a different dialog going on: "*There's no way I'm trading my car for some clap trap. I just got rid of one of those less than a year ago! Plus, I don't think saving a couple of hundred dollars is even worth it, it doesn't make a dent in the problem.*"

He was building some steam with his argument, but eventually he had to admit to himself that if he were really going to follow the *Creed* and move on to step number two, that even a couple of hundred dollars would count towards the objective of '*spending less*'.

Bertram believed he could do it and thought that was probably important. But his car was almost new and he felt like it was important that clients see him a certain way – like a successful equal instead of a whippersnapper kid. "*There's got to be another way to do this,*" he resolved.

Bertram pulled up in front of his parent's house and parked on the street so he didn't block them in. It was weird to see the *'For Sale'* sign in front of Bessie's house and his heart felt heavy as he thought about Bessie and her mom. He sat back against his seat and considered the significance of the changes in their life, taking a moment to think about his childhood and to realize that he was beginning to have feelings for Bessie that he didn't fully understand.

He popped in to say, "Hi," to his mom and dad and spent a few minutes catching up before going over to Bessie's house, probably for the last time, and ringing her doorbell. Bessie greeted him with a big smile and a warm hug, holding him close. Bertram looked around at the chaos of boxes, books and odds and ends in the living room, shaking his head a little to clear it. "Man, you guys are really leaving," he said. "I didn't really put it together until today."

Bessie gave a shrug of resignation. "I'm just ready to move on at this point. The crying is over and I'm ready for the next phase… I'm more worried about my mom adjusting, but she always handles these kinds of things better than me," she said with a laugh.

Bertram laughed with her, remembering all sorts of stories from their childhood that corroborated that fact. Bessie's mom was one of those people who just seemed to be able to float through life with a happy, practical, and tranquil view on everything, no matter how intense the situation. "Will you miss living with her?" Bertram wondered.

Bessie turned to him and said more than a thousand words with a simple nod of her head. Tying her long hair back with a band that she fished out of her back pocket, Bessie lightened the moment with a discussion of where they should eat.

They agreed on a newish place that served awesome burgers and salads, although Bertram suggested Holman's, the only fine-dining place in Weaver, secretly hoping Bessie would want something more casual so the bill would be manageable. They were walking towards his car when Bessie made the suggestion that they walk instead, the beautiful evening air making it an easy sell.

The restaurant was packed and both the food and service were way better than Bertram had expected – becoming accustomed to the higher-end places in the city made him a little choosier about restaurant experiences, generally. Conversation was easy and they lingered for a while, sharing a slice of carrot cake at the end. They bumped into multiple people they both knew which was both nice and somewhat distracting, taking a little away from the flow of their discussion.

On the walk home, Bertram decided he'd test the waters and see if Bessie was feeling anything about him, not really sure how the rules worked when the stakes were higher and something might actually turn into a relationship. "That was fun," he offered. "That place is great."

Bessie nodded and laughed. "You seemed a little flustered with all of those people constantly coming up to say 'hi' – you need to get back here more often," she teased.

Bertram stopped for a second, startling Bessie a bit. "It's funny," he said, looking right at her in hopes of reading her mind, "that's exactly what I was thinking."

It was already dark, but a wisp of a cloud passed over Bessie's face. She smiled, but not with much conviction and they walked in the quiet night for a moment or two. "Bertram," she said finally, "I was totally in love with you when we were kids. Totally and completely. I often thought about us as adults, living in town, maybe even making a family of our own. The trouble was, we were so different. By the time we got to high school you were very focused on sports and hung with the 'in' crowd and, well, I couldn't have cared less about those things. I've always wanted a simple life and you've wanted something bigger. And now, you've accomplished some of those goals… But for me, I have a desire to live here, teach kids, make a little life, and maybe start a family one day. I don't want or need anything fancy… In fact, I've resolved to let the experience with what happened after my dad's death be something that never happens to me again. Honestly, I'm way more attracted to security than anything else…"

She let that linger.

"I still… like you… a lot. I just don't see how a guy with a big job in the city and a flashy BMW fits into that picture?" She tried to joke and lighten the blow.

Bertram tried to hide his disappointment and was surprised how much hearing Bessie turn him down flat felt like someone hit him with a battering ram. The rejection having included a reference to the BMW that Norman had suggested he should sell made him feel even worse. He wasn't used to 'no' and he wasn't used to strongly wanting a 'yes' either.

He considered his response as they walked, the streetlights glowing like giant sentries. "Bessie… I'm not sure how to say this, but I'm, well, I'm hoping that maybe we could keep seeing each other and that some of the things I'm working on in my own life might… Maybe you'll start to feel differently about who you think I am."

He paused, not sure about what he was going to say next.

"The truth is, I can't stop thinking about you since we bumped into each other and had Chinese food together. And what's more, I've been working on *'adjusting my expectations'* and *'spending less'* so I can have a better life," he said, exaggerating a bit and turning on the charm. "Can we just let things keep unfolding and see how you feel?" He held his breath a little.

Bessie didn't answer immediately and they walked up the porch stairs to her front door. The house was bright inside and the sounds of a Haydn string quartet leaked through the lath and plaster walls. "Mom's blasting the classical again," Bessie said laughing, Bertram joining her.

Bessie turned and gave Bertram a big hug. "I loved our dinner. You really are someone I care about… a lot. But I don't want to lead you on, especially since we have the physical distance between us. I'm happy to see you again, just know that I don't see how we could get past some of the things I've shared."

Bertram was happy not to get an outright 'no'. "Ok, I can live with that. And yes, I understand that the odds aren't in my favor," he said.

Bessie laughed and thanked him for the evening, pulling the door shut behind her as she entered the house.

Bertram called Norman that Sunday and asked if they could grab a few minutes in the morning before work the following day. Norman usually brought his coffee from home and suggested that Bertram bring a mug down so they could take a walk around the park, talk, and sip their coffee.

Bertram was right on time and he and Norman headed out onto the quiet sidewalk. "Hey, Norman, before we go, can I show you something?" Bertram asked a little mysteriously.

"Sure, what's up?" Norman asked. They reentered the complex from the street entrance to the garage and Bertram pushed a button in his pocket. A tidy dark-green sedan chirped to signal its presence and Norman turned to smile at Bertram over his shoulder while ambling over to the car. "It's a beauty," Norman said with genuine appreciation.

Bertram couldn't help but laugh out loud. "Not sure I'd go that far, but you were right. Sylvia figured out how to save me over two hundred and fifty dollars per month and reduced the term of the loan to four years instead of the six-year lease I was in. It definitely was a good decision and the car... well, it's not awful," Bertram acknowledged. The car was Hyundai sedan with about twenty-four thousand miles; it was well-equipped, had been well taken care of and looked far less than its four years of age.

"What made you decide to pull the trigger?" Norman asked.

"Let's take that walk," Bertram suggested.

Norman, who had been sitting in the driver's seat – he had to move the seat all the way back to fit and now was trying to approximate its original location – closed the door and fell in with Bertram. They walked to the park and turned towards the rose garden, hummingbirds already visible, darting in and out of orbit around the colorful flowers.

"I'm really serious about the '*Money-Strong Creed*' and committed to making it a part of my life. I didn't tell you this, but I've been seeing someone that I think I really like and..." Bertram trailed off.

Norman tried to hide a grin. "And...?" he encouraged.

"Well, she has had some financial trauma in her life. Her father died and left her and her mother with a pretty difficult situation, which she was able to navigate but coupled with her much less..." Bertram searched for a word... "materialistic way of thinking about life. She's made it pretty clear that my current lifestyle isn't for her. It kind of was like a tipping point for me."

Norman was listening intently and his brow furrowed. "So,

Bertram, what if you get yourself *Money-Strong* and this young lady still isn't interested…? Will that set you back or are you doing this for yourself?" he asked without judgment.

"Honestly, I'm committed to being *Money-Strong*. I've played around enough… not just with relationships, but with my identity. I feel like I need to change the way I view the world and give myself a stronger foundation. When I do that, good things happen. When I let my ego and competitive drive take over, I mess things up. I need this change." Bertram seemed more resolute than Norman had ever seen him and it was clear he'd been thinking a lot about it.

"That's really good to hear. And what's also good news is that once you get your apartment situation squared away, you'll have completed the first two steps of the *Money-Strong Creed*… '*Adjust your expectations*' and '*spending less*' will be almost in the bag," Norman said encouragingly.

Bertram cocked his head. "Almost?" he challenged. "I will have saved over one thousand eight hundred dollars per month by '*spending less*' – won't that count as winning?"

They had turned around and could see the oversized windows of the upper-floor apartments of the building from where they were standing, slowing their pace just a little.

"'*Spending less*' is a way of living, not just an event," Norman explained. "Yes, lowering your rent and trading in your car are amazing examples of the '*spending less*' mindset, but it's something you have to think about every day and try to use even when the stakes are lower. For example, today, we could have met at a coffee shop but instead we brought coffee from home and saved about three dollars each. It's those little decisions that we have to be mindful of, and they come up every single day." Norman looked at Bertram to see if he was comprehending.

"I see what you mean. It's a mindset… almost like training is for your physical body. Just like I have to put in the reps in my workout to stay fit, I have to find many ways to spend less in all areas of my life," Bertram thought out loud.

"Yes, it's a daily process and requires real commitment, just like physical fitness. It's also a way of life, just like being healthy. If you go to the gym all of the time but eat double bacon cheeseburgers and wash them down with a large soda, it kind of defeats the purpose. *'Spending less'* is the same. If you save money on your housing and lower your car payment but go out to eat at fancy restaurants or take extravagant vacations all of the time, there's no gain. In order to achieve the *'spending less'* milestone, you've got to be more choosy about everything you do," Norman said, expanding on the idea.

"Man, it sounds like I need to shave my head and wear a toga or something," Bertram said half-joking. "How am I supposed to have any fun? I mean, can I *ever* do something that might cost some money?"

Norman laughed. "Of course you can… so long as it doesn't get in the way of the next three parts of the *Creed* – *'obey the one-month rule'*, *'eliminate debt'*, or *'save the difference'*. *'Spending less'* just means that you work to be conscious of your spending every day, and it's just that a 'treat' needs to be the exception and not the rule." Bertram looked a little defeated. "It's easier than it sounds, you've already made big progress," Norman said reassuringly. Then he put his arm on Bertram's shoulder conspiratorially and said, "Now, why don't you tell me about this nice young lady? She must be something special…"

With a little breathing room from his lower car payment, Bertram started trying to figure out how to get out of his current apartment lease. He had made a solid commitment to himself that he was going to stick to the *Creed*, which meant that he also had to start working on the third step to '*obey the one-month rule*' in order to begin to '*eliminate debt*'. This felt pretty daunting, but Bertram knew he could make a big dent once he got himself out from under the large lease payment and he put all of his considerable determination and drive into making that happen.

Norman had given him the contact name of the building's property-management company and they were helpful to a point. The woman who managed the building said that she'd be happy to enter into a new lease with a new tenant – so long as that tenant qualified to their credit standards. She also made it clear that Bertram would be solely responsible for finding the new tenant and reminded him subtly that he needed to continue to pay on time during the process. He resisted the urge to snap at her, knowing that it wasn't her fault that his finances were a mess and that he may need her help at some point, and got to work finding someone who wanted a seriously killer luxury apartment.

Late one Friday, Bertram was nursing a beer at his kitchen counter after failing to convince Bessie to have dinner with him. She had just moved into her new place and was still getting settled, which he thought was probably an excuse and was trying unsuccessfully not to dwell on it. In the midst of feeling sorry for himself, he suddenly came upon an idea that seemed both obvious and scary at the same time. He had tons of social media friends and followers, many of whom lived close by and were similar in age – why not advertise his place online? Bertram recognized that this exposed him to a lot of questions and could be embarrassing, but he was serious enough about freeing himself from the burden that he was willing to take that chance. He put together a solid video, some good pictures that captured the beauty of the views and the furnishings, a real-estate agent-worthy description, and after taking a deep breath, put the ad up live.

When he got back from the gym Saturday morning, his phone started to chirp. By one o'clock he had at least four solid leads from people who wanted to see his place and had scheduled a few tours for the next day. He scurried around trying to make the place look a little more presentable and took a minute to check in with Norman, reaching him on his mobile. "Hey, Norman, sorry to bug you on your day off, but I need a little direction on something. You have a minute?" Bertram hoped he hadn't overstepped.

"Hi, Bertram, no problem at all. You've saved me from mowing the grass. Irma's been bugging me for a week and I'm happy to put it off as long as I can," Norman replied, sounding impish.

Bertram could practically see Irma shaking her head at Norman in the background. "Glad to help out," he joked. "I've got some interest in the apartment, and I even have a few people coming to see it on Sunday... but I'm not sure what to do from there. The property manager had told me the tenant would need to qualify and I'm thinking there's something I can do to help that along if someone is serious... but not sure what that is." Bertram suddenly wondered why he thought Norman would have any better of an idea than him.

"Oh, that's good news for sure. Let me see if I can get a hold of Archie and he can bring you some applications. All you have to do is get the filled-out application to the property manager and they'll do the rest," Norman said, referring to the other doorman who usually covered weekends when he was out.

"That's great, thanks Norman," Bertram said, relieved. "I'll let you get back to avoiding your chores," he ribbed.

"Actually, I've been talking to Irma and we were wondering if you'd like to come back over for dinner at the end of the summer? Maybe another Sunday?"

Bertram couldn't pass up a chance to hang with one of his friends and eat some of the best food he'd ever had in his life, and thanked Norman enthusiastically for the invitation. They settled on a date at the end of August.

"Say, Bertram, do you want to invite your lady friend, Bessie, to join us? You're welcome to…"

Bertram thanked Norman but admitted that he wasn't sure Bessie was going to want to take that kind of a step at this point.

"Well, you just let her know she's welcome, and that we'd love to meet her," Norman said, and they signed off.

The summer sun was setting the next evening and Bertram was quietly taking in the view from his balcony. The day had gone very well – three of the four people who came through the apartment filled out applications and he figured that over the next week or so, he'd be moving down to his new closet on the sixth floor.

Bertram sighed and sat back on his lounge chair, thankful that he'd made so much progress on his financial challenges and thinking about Bessie despite his best efforts. As the last tiny bit of sunlight reflected off of the glass buildings around him and the lake in the middle of the park, he wondered to himself if that little ache tugging at his heart like a paperweight might be what love feels like. Whatever the case, he knew it only went away when he was talking to Bessie or with her, and since she didn't seem to feel the same way, he wasn't sure what on earth he was going to do about it.

———

Bertram was dragging. He'd moved all weekend, helping the various people who had bought his furniture lug it to their waiting cars and trucks and then moving the few belongings that remained to his new place. He'd made a little money selling all of the stuff he'd acquired to furnish the big apartment but it wasn't close to enough to pay off the credit-card balance that remained from when he bought it. Despite that, he was happy to be done with the whole chapter and was set up enough in his new place that he was able to find his coffee maker and Thermos which was all he needed to get through his work day.

Mr. Vaughan had scheduled Bertram's mid-year sales review for that day and Bertram was ready, even though the timing wasn't perfect. He and his team had backfilled a reasonable portion of the NetCore losses and the first six months of the year were still slightly ahead of the prior year. While he didn't feel great about the results, Bertram figured with the pipeline they had, he had a whiff of a chance to still meet the growth goals set for him.

They met in the conference room around the lunch hour and Vaughan had ordered some food for them. Bertram was a little surprised since it wasn't Mr. Vaughan's style to think about things like eating, or small talk, or other little things that humans typically appreciate. After getting settled with their sandwiches, Mr. Vaughan got right to it. "Looks like you've made some pretty good progress since losing NetCore," he said with a hint of surprise. "That's good news."

"Yes, well, we still have a lot of work to do to end the year how we need it to look," Bertram replied, taken off guard by the praise. "We are pushing hard to make the fourth quarter a big one and it will likely be a nail-biter."

Vaughan took a last bite of his ham and cheese and a

couple of sips from his water bottle. "Yes, I see that. Well, good work. I think you can do it. I'm more impressed with you than I thought." Vaughan looked at Bertram as if he was solving a crossword puzzle.

Bertram laughed. "Thanks, I guess?" he offered.

"I had pegged you as one of those athletes who had skated by on his charm through a lot of his childhood and had turned from a frat boy to a party boy once he got into the real world. Maybe I was wrong about that," Mr. Vaughan said, by way of explanation. "I see the effort you're putting in and you've proven you can handle some adversity. Keep up the good work." Vaughan was tidying up his area and had stood to leave. Bertram wasn't done eating and Vaughan waved him back down to his chair, "Take your time... I want to take a walk since I didn't get to the gym this morning. I'll see you later." Vaughan threw his garbage in the trash and started to walk out. "Oh, I almost forgot," he said from the doorway. "I added a small salary bump to your check effective immediately. It's not much, more of a vote of confidence than anything, but I think you've earned it. Have a good week." Vaughan didn't wait for a response and headed briskly towards the elevator.

Back in his office, Bertram thought it might be time to figure out how to attack his debt. He figured that between the savings he'd accomplished by trading in his car, including a lower insurance bill, his rent reduction, and some of the other spending habits he'd changed, he could make fairly good progress on eliminating his debt. Doing some quick math, he figured that he could be completely debt free with the exception of his car in about eight months. Noodling a little further, it seemed it might take another year and a half after that to pay off his car loan.

While this didn't seem like forever, it wasn't fast enough for Bertram. He thought that one important way to get Bessie's attention would be to prove himself to be *Money-Strong*. He knew that the changes he'd made already would help, but that Bessie was looking for something more than just a superficial change of residence – she wanted him to be financially stable and have a similar mindset as she had about security. He'd talked to Simon and a couple of his other closer friends about her, a big step for a self-avowed bachelor and party animal, and after razzing him for an appropriate amount of time, they all came to the same conclusion: Bertram needed to prove that he had fundamentally changed, not just that he'd made changes.

–––

Bertram was having a frustrating day. On the one hand, he'd gotten his first paycheck after his new raise went into effect and was pleasantly surprised to find that he was earning about three hundred dollars per month more after taxes. Excited by this, he resolved to add the whole amount of the raise every month towards '*eliminating debt*', figuring it would make a huge impact.

Early that morning, Bertram started looking a little more deeply at the amounts he owed, closely scrutinizing his credit-card and car-loan balances and he came to a very disappointing conclusion. Even if he put every single dollar of extra cash that he'd freed up by '*spending less*' into '*eliminating debt*', and added his recent raise, he was still almost two years away from being able to stash a single dollar in savings.

Although he hadn't talked with Bessie about it in detail, Bertram knew enough to realize that she wouldn't feel remotely comfortable getting serious about their relationship if he had no savings, even if he was debt-free. He wasn't sure she would be interested in him even if he had a large amount of savings, but he was sure she wouldn't be interested at all if he had nothing saved whatsoever. The problem was, no matter how he rearranged the math, he couldn't figure out how to get it paid off earlier. Seeing all of the results of his loose spending habits laid out right before his eyes made him feel a little hopeless, taking him back to the feeling he had before he had trimmed his car payment and switched apartments. Bertram wasn't sure what he was going to do, but one thing was for sure, once he got out of debt, he was going to be sure never to get back into it.

The other thing that was gnawing at Bertram was his inability to get Bessie to commit to going on another date. He wasn't used to people rejecting him generally, and he wasn't sure how to handle it. Bertram was worried that if he pushed too hard, she might just shut down completely. As it stood, they were having some good phone conversations and were texting often. Against his inclination to be even more proactive, he thought hanging back a bit was the right strategy.

He was feeling a little awkward that he hadn't let Norman know about whether Bessie would join him for dinner. Bertram had asked her about it the last time they had spoken on the phone but she was just about to start her new teaching job and was busy getting her classroom set up before the kids came back from summer vacation. She had been non-committal at the time and hadn't returned his call from yesterday, which was somewhat unusual.

Bertram sighed and pushed back from the small table in the kitchen where he tended to work when he was home. After a week or so of adjustment shock, he found he liked his little studio. He'd even had a few of his friends over to watch the Wimbledon finals and even though it was nothing near his epic blowouts, it was still a lot of fun.

He figured a change of scenery would brighten his mood so he decided he'd take a long walk and try to enjoy the still-tolerable, late summer-morning weather before it got too steamy. His phone started to ring before he got out the door and seeing that it was Bessie, he thought he'd stay put so his cellphone service didn't make the call choppy. "Hi there!" he said, without further introduction.

"Hey, Bertram, how are you?" Bessie asked, sounding a little weary.

"Good, good, everything ok with you?" he inquired, hoping his cheery voice might give her a lift.

"Yes, everything's fine, just busy getting everything finalized at school. I'm nervous and excited – almost like I used to feel before school started when we were kids. I must admit that getting the lesson plans put together and everything has been really fun, but it's also been a lot more work that I expected."

"Those kids are lucky to have you as their teacher – you'll be one of the favorites right out of the gate," Bertram said with conviction. He took a deep breath. "So Bessie… what are you doing later today? Do you want to go on a picnic?"

The idea came completely out of the blue but he thought it might be interesting and safe enough that she just might say yes. There was a little pause through which he thought he spied a ray or two of hope.

"Bertram. I've got to tell you that I've sort of been seeing someone. I'm not sure that it's very serious, and we've only gone out a few times, but I didn't want to lead you on. You know that I care about you… and you know that your lifestyle, well, it scares me, I guess. I'm not sure that us having more time together right now is a great idea." She spoke softly as if that would make the news easier to hear.

Bertram's head spun and he felt a little clammy. He took a few more deep breaths and sat down, working very hard not to react in a way that could scare Bessie off. "Bess… I… I… understand," was all he could manage at first, knowing full well that he felt the exact opposite of what he was saying. He took a moment to collect his thoughts. "Bessie, you know that friend of mine, Norman, I've told you about? The one who invited us to dinner in a couple of weeks?"

"Yes, I remember," Bessie replied.

"I'm hoping you'll come, even if it's clear that you feel that we're just friends. I've been learning so much from him... I've been getting help from him to get my finances in order. I'm not there yet, but he introduced me to something called the '*Money-Strong Creed*' which has made a big impact so far. I recognize that you're frightened by the way I've handled myself in the past, and I know that you are seeing someone else. I also know that my goal of winning you over is a long shot. Regardless, it would mean a lot to me if you met him and his wife, Irma. No strings or obligations. Really, just as friends." He could almost see Bessie looking at him with that scrunched-up expression that she used to use when she thought he was trying to pull one over on her.

She didn't respond for a moment, long enough that Bertram wasn't sure she was even still on the line. "Ok, Bertram," she said with a sigh, sounding a little exasperated. "I'll come, but only under the condition that you are clear that I'm coming to support you, not as your girlfriend. I don't want them feeling awkward or like they have to try to matchmake for us..." She trailed off.

"Of course, of course." Bertram felt like he just got his team in field goal position and within sight of the lead. "I'll make sure they know what's up and stuff. I really appreciate you doing this." They discussed logistics and said goodbye, agreeing to meet at Norman and Irma's since it was towards Weaver if they were coming from the city.

Bertram wasn't sure whether he felt better or worse than before the call, but decided he was going to focus on the positive and that his team was still in the game. From where Bertram was standing, however, the stakes on getting rid of his debt more quickly had just gone way, way up.

Bertram resisted the urge to call Norman and bug him over the weekend but he rang down to the bell stand first thing Monday to see if Norman wanted a refill on his coffee and could chat for a minute. Norman said that he hadn't ploughed through his Thermos yet but would love to chat.

They greeted each other warmly with a big hug and caught up a little before Bertram swung around to the issue at hand. Once he got rolling, Bertram talked quickly, fearing interruption by the typical steady flow of tenants heading out to work on a Monday who always wanted to say hello to Norman.

Bertram laid out his debt situation, showing Norman all the numbers he had been working on, stressing the importance of paying the loans off earlier so that he could begin to '*save the difference*', but also sharing his inability to find a way to do that.

"Wow, that was a lot to take in," Norman said, grinning and shaking his head. "You're like a speed racer!"

Bertram laughed at himself. "Yeah, I've been thinking about pretty much nothing else the last forty-eight hours or so," he admitted, leaving out the part about Bessie for the moment.

"It's awesome that you've put so much thought into the fourth step of '*eliminating debt*', but you're skipping one of the most important steps of all: '*obey the one-month rule*'," Norman reminded Bertram.

Bertram looked like someone just called a foul on him from the stands. "I did? I guess… maybe you're right; it seems more important to just get my debt paid off, I mean, I've piled up quite a bit of it and I pay a lot of interest every month, plus I have a decent job, so…"

Norman nodded his head slowly. "You're right – you have a great job and a reasonably large amount of debt, but the *'one-month rule'* is non-negotiable. How it works is, whatever your take home pay is in one month, you put that amount away for a rainy day. Once that's done, you leave it alone in a savings account and you can waltz right on over to step four: *'eliminating debt'*. This little savings plan is crucial because if you lose your job… or a big account or whatever… it doesn't cause you to have an immediate financial emergency. Later, you'll save quite a bit more… but this is a safety net that will protect you from the unexpected things life throws at you."

Bertram was clearly disappointed that he couldn't dive right into paying off his debts since he already found that *'eliminating debt'* would take longer than he'd hoped.

Norman, sensing his disappointment, changed the subject a bit. "Bertram, do you get your paychecks directly deposited into your checking account?"

"Yes, we get paid on the fifth and the twentieth," Bertram replied.

"Ok, perfect. Would you mind opening the banking app on your phone? I'm going to show you something that will make the *'one-month rule'* really simple," Norman said reassuringly. Bertram fiddled with his phone for a moment and pulled up his account summary. "Ok, now, go to your checking-account deposits and look for last month's payroll deposits… There should be two: one on the fifth and one on the twentieth. Do you see them?" Bertram acknowledged that he did. "Great," Norman said, opening up the calculator app on his phone. "Can you please give me both of those numbers?" Norman punched in Bertram's figures, adding the two numbers together. "Based upon that, your one-month safety net is right at four thousand two hundred dollars. Then, what that means is, before you move on to start *'eliminating debt'* you need to save four thousand, two hundred dollars and stash it away."

Bertram looked dejected. "That will take a few months," he said, almost to himself.

"When Irma and I were just married, we saved and scrimped and put together just enough money to buy a tiny little house over where all the warehouses are now, just north of the city. Back then, it was old, cheap housing but it was a clean, safe neighborhood, full of mostly young, hard-working people like us. You know where I mean?"

Bertram shook his head, only vaguely understanding. "I'm not sure – you mean where all of the trucking and logistics warehouses are, over by the old stadium?"

"Yes, that's right. There used to be a nice little neighborhood of older homes there, back in the day. Anyway, Irma and I didn't have kids yet and she had a good job as a staff accountant for a commercial kitchen supply company that had been around forever and a day. Between my job with Mr. Sykes and Irma's job, we could afford to live a modest lifestyle, just like the '*Money-Strong Creed*' dictates."

Bertram listened attentively.

"One day, Irma was waiting for me with dinner already done and keeping warm in the oven when I got home. This was unusual since we usually arrived home around the same time and it was my turn to cook dinner. Turns out, her company was sold and the new owners laid off all of the support staff at the same time, sending over thirty-five people home, just like Irma, that very day. She was upset and I was too; she enjoyed her job and the people she worked with, plus her income helped us keep up with our savings plan and pay some of our other bills.

"With a brand-new mortgage, it could easily have been a serious problem for us. But as it turned out, since we had properly obeyed the '*one-month rule*', we had a cushion consisting of a total of one month of our combined take-home pay. Even when we were shopping for a house, we were careful not to consider the *'one-month rule'* money as available in any way… all of our down payment and any other purchase expenses had to come from our *'save the difference'* money. With our *'one-month rule'* safety net and a little further belt-tightening, we were able to ride out her job search without much discomfort and without having to borrow money. The *'one-month rule'* is a major stress-reliever when things happen that you don't count on."

Bertram absorbed the story and had to admit that the *'one-month rule'* would have made all of the difference in his own situation. If he had a month of take-home pay, he would have been able to avoid quite a few sleepless nights over his reduction in income and the vaporizing bonus he'd been counting on. "Ok, yes, I see your point. So you're saying I have to save one month of my take-home pay at four thousand two hundred dollars in order to *'obey the one-month rule'* and move on to *'eliminating debt',*" Bertram recapped, "which means I'm three months away from starting my debt-elimination plan." Bertram looked resigned to the outcome but not happy about it.

"It's actually only two full months… maybe even less if you find other ways to save your pennies," Norman pointed out. "Remember, you have $1,800 per month freed up to put into your safety-net account. After two months, you'll have $3,600, meaning only $600 left to go. So, in the third month, you'll put the final $600 into savings, giving you the $4,200 total. Once you have $4,200, you've met the *'obey the one-month rule'* objective so the $1,200 that's left over will immediately go to start *'eliminating debt'*. You'll still have $1,200 to pay down debt after giving the final $600 to your safety-net account."

"Ok, I get that, having a safety net definitely makes sense and I'll get started this month," Bertram said with conviction. "But I'm still worried that I won't be able to get my debt eliminated in any reasonable amount of time. Two years feels like forever." Bertram was still not fully ready to share his concern about Bessie and how that factored into his worries.

"Bertram, have you ever heard of something called snowballing or accelerating when it comes to paying off debts?" Norman asked. Bertram acknowledged that he hadn't. "Well, it's a great little tool and it will pay off your debts way faster than trying to pay down everything at the same time. How it works is, you take each of your balances and you list them in order from the smallest balance to the largest. The interest rate doesn't matter and how long you have left to pay isn't important either. You just take your lowest balance first and use all of the money you freed up by *'spending less'* on your apartment, auto, and other expenses, plus the income from your raise, to pay it off. Once that debt is gone, you add whatever monthly payment you had been making on that card to the amount of money you've freed up by *'spending less'*, and use that new larger total to get rid of the next smallest balance. You keep doing this until everything is paid off," Norman stated, watching Bertram to see if he comprehended it. Bertram looked a little puzzled so Norman continued.

"Let's do an example just to make it easier to follow," Norman pulled the paper containing Bertram's scribbles that he had been noodling on for the past two days over where they could both see it. "Including your raise, rent and car-payment savings, plus a few of the other things you're *'spending less'* on every month, you have a whopping $1,800 per month to pay off debt. Now, your smallest balance is your TotalElectronics Visa card, and it looks like you owe almost exactly $1,800 on that one. The payment on that card is $100 per month, a lot of which goes to interest. Using the accelerator method, you will actually be able to pay this debt off completely in your first full month of debt elimination. Remember, you'll have about $1,200 left after you fund your safety net to put towards retiring your debt, then a full month of $1,800 to pay down debt after that. So in the second month, you'll have eliminated the TotalElectronics balance of $1,800 and will have additional funds left over to start paying down the next card balance. Then, you will take the monthly payment of $100 that you no longer have to make to TotalElectronics and add it to the amount you can pay to start getting rid of the next largest debt. So now, moving forward, you have a total of $1,900 instead of $1,800 to pay towards debt number two, which in this case is your MidRiverBank Mastercard with a balance of $3,800. That card has a minimum payment of almost $200, so once you pay it off in two months, you'll add that amount to the total you can pay towards your next debt. This means that in just a few months you'll have gone from $1,800 to $2,100 available to pay down debt number three, plus, you'll have eliminated two debts completely!" Norman said enthusiastically.

Bertram was digesting the process and had a furrow in his brow. "So each time you pay a debt off, you add whatever that monthly payment was to the total you can use to pay down the next one?" he asked tentatively.

"Yes, exactly," Norman responded.

"Why wouldn't you pay off the one with the highest rate first?" Bertram asked. "It seems like that would make the most sense?"

Norman nodded. "There's nothing wrong with that approach and many people use it. The thing that makes this so much more powerful is that you can feel and see the progress as the debts fall away, and you gain the ability to quickly add more money to the total amount you're using to eliminate each successive debt. The monthly payments you've eliminated roll up into a much bigger number, acting like a turbo-charger for paying off your debts."

Bertram, nodded, doing some figuring. "If I'm right, it

looks like I'll shave almost a year off of '*eliminating debt*' entirely just by using the accelerator. Wow, that's powerful." Bertram's eyes were wide.

"I felt the same way when I first learned about it," Norman agreed. "It's pretty amazing. Oh, Donald had shared some website that I guess does all the calculations exactly if you'd like to use it," Norman scrolled through some messages. "Here it is, www.milleronmoney.com/accelerator.tool.html, I'll text it to you. Let's put your information in here and see what it looks like, just for fun," Norman suggested, clicking on the link.

Bertram showed Norman his figures and Norman tried to poke them into the screen, but his huge fingers made it slow going. "Can I help?" Bertram asked pleasantly, putting out his hand for Norman to place the phone into.

"What, you don't have all day for me to peck at this like a rooster?" Norman chuckled, happily handing his friend the phone. After a few moments, Bertram had finished pumping in all of his information and the software automatically computed the results. They looked at the report and reviewed it together.

DEBT SUMMARY

	AMOUNT OWED	INTEREST RATE	MONTHLY PAYMENT
Credit cards	$17,700	12.43%	$708.00
Auto loans	$26,000	1.9%	$486.00
Other loans	$0	0%	$0.00
Total	$43,700	6.16%	$1,194.00

SNOWBALL DEBT DETAILS

	AMOUNT OWED	INITIAL SNOWBALL MONTHLY PAYMENT*	MONTHLY PAYMENT
Credit card 1	$1,800	$1,872.00 starts in month 1	2 months
Credit card 2	$3,800	$2,038.13 starts in month 2	3 months
Credit card 3	$5,900	$2,281.66 starts in month 4	6 months
Credit card 4	$6,200	$2,508.00 starts in month 7	8 months
Auto loan 1	$26,000	$2,994.00 starts in month 9	16 months
Total	$43,700	$2,994.00	1 year & 4 months

"Looking at this, and using your current balances, you'll be done paying off the debt in only sixteen months instead of two years," Norman pointed out.

"That's amazing. I mean, that doesn't even include anything extra I can add to the total monthly amount I use to pay off the debt," Bertram said, starting to understand how powerful the system was. "Look, if I started off with $1,900 instead of $1,800, this shows me paying the whole debt off one month earlier. It's crazy how much of a difference $100 makes!" Bertram said excitedly.

"Now you've got the hang of it," Norman said, like a fan rooting from the sidelines.

"Every little bit makes a big impact," Bertram said with some hope in his voice. "Awesome. Thanks, Norman." He took a moment to process what Norman had taught him as the doorman busied himself with a few quick morning pleasantries with passing tenants.

Once Norman was finished, Bertram told him about Bessie, sharing the whole conversation, even though he didn't usually feel comfortable sharing rejection with anyone. "So that's about it," Bertram said by way of an ending, punctuating his feeling of powerlessness with a cross between a head toss and a shrug.

Norman patted his friend's shoulder. "Don't give up... I have a feeling you can win this one. Just be yourself, stay honest with her and keep doing the work of becoming '*Money-Strong*'. She'll come around... I know she will. Even if she doesn't, not too long from now, you'll end up free from the trap of money anxiety and stress that most people have their whole lives. That's a big win, too..." Norman said reassuringly.

Bertram nodded and wished Norman a good day, needing to get a move on if he was going to get to the office on time.

The red door opened and Irma was there to greet them both with warm hugs, Bessie visibly calming the instant she was inside of Irma's arms. "Welcome, welcome!" Irma said with obvious pleasure, thanking Bessie for the jade plant she had brought and Bertram for the nice bottle of Cabernet he'd pulled from his closet, a remnant of his former spending habits. They could hear Norman's voice from somewhere deeper in the house before they could see him, drying his hands as he stepped out of the kitchen.

"Hello, hello and welcome!" Norman greeted them both warmly, giving Bertram his standard bear hug.

"Oh my..." Bessie said the instant she saw Norman, looking like she'd just won a Grammy but had no idea she was in the running. "Mr. Price? Is that you? I... I can't believe it." Bessie's eyes were damp as she gave Norman a big hug.

"I wondered if you might be the very same girl I had met at the coffee shop that day – Bessie is such an uncommon name. I am sure glad it is…" Norman said.

Bessie took a white linen handkerchief from her purse and dabbed at her eyes. "I feel badly that I never gave this back; it has been a good-luck charm and just couldn't let it go," she said laughing, embarrassed at herself.

The finely threaded fabric with the initials '*NP*' came in handy yet again and Norman laughed out loud.

"Well, it would seem you've gotten good use out of it and I certainly haven't missed it," he said convincingly.

Bertram, clearly confused, was trying to figure out how Norman and Bessie knew each other, while Irma looked as if these types of reunions were a daily occurrence. They wandered from the foyer into the kitchen and Bessie explained to Irma and Bertram how she had come to know Norman.

"Wow, that's crazy," Bertram said once Bessie told the whole story, still surprised by the twist of events. "So Norman was the one who helped you get your financial life together as well…" he marveled out loud, looking at his friend with a mixture of awe and disbelief.

"Norman has all sorts of people around here that feel that way about him," Irma said with some pride. "He is a lot smarter than he looks," she added, throwing her husband a flirtatious smile.

Norman flushed a little at the attention, obviously uncomfortable with any public praise. "I'm just doing my duty, just doing my duty, you know that," he said humbly.

Bertram knew what Norman meant and told a little of the story about how he had won Irma and the '*Money-Strong Creed*' so that Bessie was in on the joke. Bessie wandered over and gave Norman a sideways hug and they all returned to typical suburban small talk for a few moments.

While Irma and Bessie chatted in the kitchen, Norman

motioned Bertram to follow him with his head. "No way Irma's putting us all to work... poor Bessie doesn't know what she's in for," Norman said quietly to Bertram as they snuck away.

"Norman," Irma called sternly as they slid out into the hallway.

Norman smiled at Bertram. "She's too quick for me!" he joked conspiratorially. "Yes, ma'am?"

"Don't think this means you won't need to come back to cut that rib... I know your tricks..." She was laughing but not joking.

"No problem, just call me when you need me to take it out..." Norman said, relieved that she didn't have a whole list for him.

They went into the study and Bertram was again struck by the peaceful elegance of it. On the desk was a gold box, covered in filigree with a white bow on it, the only thing on an otherwise spotless desktop.

Norman pushed the box toward Bertram without saying anything. Not fully understanding, Bertram looked at Norman and pointed at his own chest. "For me?" he asked, genuinely surprised.

"Yes, I've been excited to give it to you. Please, open it..." Norman said, making a rolling motion with his hand.

"Wow, ok, thanks." Bertram wasn't used to getting gifts, especially outside of a birthday or the holidays.

Inside the filigree box was a bed of pillowed white tissue paper and something heavy like a book wrapped with tissue that was golden in color. Bertram carefully unwrapped the item revealing a deeply stained oil-rubbed maple plaque, beautiful and virtually identical to the one containing the 'Money-Strong Creed' that hung behind Norman. The brass on the front was etched just like Norman's, but this plaque was personalized with Bertram's name and was missing the final item – instead of *'save the difference'*, there was a blank space, large enough for the letters to fit but without the writing.

Bertram held it in his hands for a moment before looking at his friend. "Thank you so much, Norman. This is truly gorgeous, and I'm really honored that you did this for me," he said openly and genuinely.

Norman nodded with a little spark in his eye, not saying a word. After a moment, Norman stood up and sat back against the credenza. "You probably want to know why the final line of the *Creed* is missing," Norman said. Bertram nodded that he did. "By now, you've either completed the other four steps or are well on your way. When you've finished *'eliminating debt'* and are solidly at the point where you're *'saving the difference'*, I'm going to take you to the shop out back and show you how to engrave the last part yourself; just like what was done for me when I got mine so many years ago."

Bertram was rarely emotional, but he was having a hard time choking back tears. He sat still for a moment. "You don't have another one of those fancy handkerchiefs do you?" he asked, half-joking.

"Dinner was amazing," Bessie said, barely able to believe how delicious the meal was. "Bertram told me to expect something out of this world but, Irma, I can't believe how great a cook you are."

Norman asked Bertram to help him clear the dinner dishes and they put on some fresh coffee, Norman showing Bertram how to grind the beans properly for the antique French press. Bertram couldn't help but snoop around the oven which clearly was in the final throes of baking something blissful for dessert. Norman chuckled at Bertram who was trying to get a good look at things without opening the oven door and blowing his cover. "I'll let it be a surprise, but I sure hope you've saved room," Norman chided.

Bertram shook his head and patted his stomach. "There's

not much room in there but I won't let that stop me," he said emphatically. "No way I'm missing out on that heavenly creation, whatever it may be!"

The four of them sat around sipping their coffee and chatting for a while, enjoying each other and the leisurely pace of a great Sunday evening in the Indian summer.

"Bertram tells me you are officially a teacher now," Norman said to Bessie admiringly. "That's really hard work but something tells me you're going to be great at it."

Bessie smiled somewhat demurely, "I sure hope so," she said. "Tomorrow is actually the first official day of school but the kids don't arrive until Wednesday morning. We do two days of in-service training with the other teachers and then the onslaught begins."

"What made you decide to be a teacher?" Irma asked. "Was it something you always wanted to do?"

Bessie took a sip of her coffee and set it carefully back in the simply designed but elegantly patterned saucer. "Honestly, it was a second choice for me. Teaching seemed like it could be interesting, but mostly, I wanted to be a writer when I was growing up. I wrote all the time when I was younger, at least all of the time when I wasn't reading." Everyone laughed. Bessie felt the need to explain further. "When I was choosing a university, I mostly looked for one with a great creative-writing program and was lucky enough to get into Swarthmore. I learned a ton there and while most of the kids partied, I stayed behind and wrote. I wrote a number of short stories and two plays, getting some encouragement and great instruction which pushed me to keep going."

Bessie did a quick attention and interest check – she wasn't used to monopolizing the conversation. Everyone was fully locked into her, clearly wanting to hear more, which felt encouraging. "I submitted some of my work, at my writing advisor's request, to a few publications and somehow got two of my stories published in a small literary journal which felt great." She paused a moment. "After graduation, I decided to work at the kind of job which didn't require much thinking so I could reserve my mental energy for writing. I waited tables and tended bar, both of which paid well enough for me to pay the rent on the tiny place I lived in and weren't creatively demanding. I spent the mornings and most afternoons writing, picking up just enough shifts to make ends meet. I was working on a novel and felt fairly good about my progress.

"Once it was ready enough, I started to submit a few sample chapters and a book proposal to agents with the guidance of two of my former college professors who were kind enough to mentor me even after school. For almost a year I diligently submitted the proposal to agencies and continued to write, finishing the book and starting on a rewrite. Unfortunately, I appeared to be better at getting rejections than at writing fiction, and the rejections started to pile up. I started to lose a little faith in myself and then…" Bessie made a small gesture of resignation with her hands… "my father died."

Irma patted Bessie's arm and let her hand rest there. Bessie reached over with her other arm and gave Irma's hand a squeeze, leaving her hand on top of Irma's. "I think the combination of the rejections and my dad's death made it clear to me that my life needed to head in a different direction. When I came back home to help my mom, I got a job in a café where I had worked before and tried to continue to write. But my heart wasn't in it. I had no attention span either; our bleak financial situation crowded my thoughts and it seemed like it was time to move on and become an adult. So, I enrolled in state college's credential program and redrafted my plan a little. I had always thought teaching could be fun and I love kids. Plus, the security and the benefits, along with a real retirement plan made teaching that much more appealing.

Not to mention having the summers free – that's a big plus and I'm thankful our district isn't year-round." Bessie smiled, hoping to brighten the mood. "Sorry, that was probably too much information."

"Do you think you might get back to writing at some point?" Norman asked. "Sounds like you were really terrific at it."

Bessie laughed. "Well, about fifty agents would disagree with you, but yes, it's possible that some day I'll feel the desire to write again. For now, I'm working on getting my life re-stabilized and putting my attention and energy into my new career path. I'm nervous about teaching but I'm also excited and eager to learn how to do it well. Now that the financial part of my life is finally stable, I'm excited to be able to bring some focus to something meaningful to me." Norman nodded understandingly.

Irma brought the dessert to the table in individual portions. The plates were mounded with an exquisitely fragrant peach cobbler made with late-summer Ohio peaches and a scoop of handmade vanilla ice cream.

"Oh my lord," Bessie said, shaking her head. "I'm never leaving!"

Everyone laughed and grew quiet as they enjoyed the otherworldly flavors, almost complete silence falling over the table with the exception of the occasional scrape of a spoon or a random grunt or groan of culinary pleasure. Once the dessert was gone, everyone looked around the table at each other, smiling contentedly, as if they'd shared an inside joke no one else could possibly understand.

"Irma and Norman, I can't thank you enough." Bessie hugged her hosts meaningfully. "You really made me feel like a part of the family." Bessie took Norman's huge hands into her comparatively tiny ones. "Norman, I have to tell you, I am so grateful for your kindness that day and your introduction to Mrs. Winslow. We never would have been able to get in the position we are in now without you." She hugged him again.

Norman waved her off. "It was really nothing at all," he said, "and Irma and I are so thankful you shared your Sunday with us, especially on your first 'school night'!"

Bertram and Bessie waved as they headed down the walkway to their respective cars, Norman and Irma lingering in the doorway and waving back, a halo-like glow behind their heads lighting the path as they went.

Bertram walked Bessie to her car and opened the door for her. "Thank you for coming," he said. "It was really special to have you meet them."

Bessie nodded. "I'm super-glad I came as well... How crazy that Norman was the Mr. Price whose chance meeting with me saved my mom and I. Sort of like an angel, that man..." She trailed off. "What's that you're holding? I've been meaning to ask you about it." Bessie motioned to the box.

"Oh, I almost forgot to show you this. Norman hasn't just been your angel... he's working on becoming mine too," Bertram said, unwrapping the *'Money-Strong Creed'* plaque.

"That's beautiful," Bessie said, moving the plaque inside the car a bit so the overhead light made it more visible.

"Yes... it is. I'm learning some things about how to live my life differently. And it's already made a huge impact," Bertram said with a note of surprise reflecting in his voice.

Bessie looked at him and smiled, then motioned with her head towards the Hyundai. "I noticed," she said. "Nice ride."

She smiled and gave Bertram a little hug, gently giving back the plaque and then sliding into her seat and starting the car. She rolled down the window. "Bertram, thanks again for making this dinner happen, I loved the evening. I've got to get back... It's late and I have a big day tomorrow."

"I know and I wish you an awesome day," Bertram said. "Will you call me and tell me how it went?"

Bessie thought about it for a moment. "Thanks for the good wishes. I'll text you at the end of the day…"

Bessie gave a little wave as she drove off, keeping the window down to let in the cooling night air, Bertram watching until the sound of her engine melted into the whir of chirping crickets.

A week before winter break, Bertram was on his way to Weaver on a snowy and frigid Friday afternoon. His brother Allen had recently moved back from New Jersey where he had been living with his wife and two girls and Bertram was anxious to see him and the kids. Allen was his oldest brother and because of their age difference, Bertram didn't know him as well as his other siblings but he'd always respected him. With his brothers and his sister spread out all over the country, having Allen a little closer was going to be nice and he had vowed to make the most of it.

It helped that Bessie's school was close to his brother's new house. Bertram had brought a small Christmas gift for her and thought he'd swing by class and surprise her with it before he headed to over to see Allen. It was after the students had been dismissed for the day and there was no one to check him in at the office so he wandered back towards where he thought Bessie's class would be. Not much had changed since he went to school at Northside Elementary and he remembered where the fourth-grade classrooms were without much difficulty. Bertram saw the colorful paintings and posters lining the walls before he arrived at Bessie's door, stopping to admire a few of them which were awfully advanced for the work of nine-year-olds. They hadn't had much time to talk lately and he was excited to see her – he was making good progress on his *'Money-Strong'* efforts and feeling like his chances with Bessie were improving.

Bertram knocked on the closed door to announce his arrival and walked into Bessie's classroom. Bessie was sitting on the edge of her desk and talking to someone that Bertram couldn't see, looking up in surprise as Bertram entered.

"Oh, hi, Bertram!" Bessie said when he walked in. "I wasn't expecting you!"

At that moment, Bertram's attention went to the back of the classroom, where Tom Sparks, a fellow teacher at Northside who Bertram and Bessie had grown up with, was standing on a ladder, taping up holiday decorations representing different religions.

Tom, seeing Bertram, turned around and waved good-naturedly. "Hey, Bertram, Merry Christmas! It's been forever… Let me finish this for the slave driver and I'll come down and say hello properly," he joked.

"Hey, Tom, no worries – don't hurt yourself," Bertram said, feeling uneasy somehow. Tom's family lived a few blocks from where Bertram and Bessie grew up in a large older stucco home with a Spanish tiled roof that always looked like it needed a facelift. While Bertram knew Tom and his two siblings well, he didn't hang out with him much as a kid. Tom tended to be bookish and shy and Bertram was always playing some sport or another. They were friendly, but they weren't friends.

"Tom was kind enough to volunteer to help me get ready for the final week of school before holiday break… We're learning about religious traditions from around the world," Bessie explained.

"Nice, that's great," Bertram said, a little jealous that he couldn't be climbing the ladder instead but working hard to cover it up.

"Would you like to set that down?" Bessie asked as she rose to give Bertram a friendly hug, pointing at the little package in his hands.

"Sure, it's actually for you…" Bertram put it on the desk, wondering if popping in unannounced may have been a mistake.

"That's so sweet… Thank you for thinking of me," Bessie said, looking a little uncomfortable.

"It's… nothing, just, anyway, Merry Christmas," Bertram said, trying to be casual and put her at ease.

Tom had extricated himself from the ladder and extended his hand to Bertram. "Good to see you," he said, shaking Bertram's hand with a genuine smile.

"Thanks, you too, Tom, it's been a long time – you look good," Bertram observed, honestly surprised at how athletic and fit Tom looked, having remembered him as a thin, gaunt nerdy kid with glasses that had frames too big for his head.

Tom chuckled. "Thanks, I've been into running for a while recently. I did a bit of intramural running in college but officially caught the race bug about four years ago and have been training more consistently… It keeps me sane with these crazy kids yelling at me from all directions." Bertram laughed.

"He's being modest," Bessie said, putting an arm around Tom as she said it. "Tom has run quite a few marathons and is fast enough that he qualified for the Boston Marathon next year."

They looked relaxed and familiar, which gave Bertram an unexpected stab of jealousy; he hoped it wasn't obvious. Before he could comment, Bessie said,

"Bertram, I have some news and since you're here, well, I thought I'd tell you about it now." Bessie spoke a little tentatively, her eyes on Bertram's face. He attempted to return the gaze in a relaxed way, but alarms were going off in his brain and body, making it very hard to stay calm.

"We've decided to get married!" Tom said enthusiastically, Bessie nodding in agreement. "Another Weaver homegrown wedding…" Tom offered, as if reporting census data, Bessie giggling nervously.

Bertram couldn't immediately respond, but when he did, he was able to congratulate them and give them each a hug before leaving them together and making a hasty exit. He felt like one of those cars at the junkyard just after the crusher had flattened it into a pancake.

Bertram sat in his car in front of Allen's house and collected himself. The snow that had fallen earlier in the day had been cleared and although it was dark, he could tell that the walkway had been shoveled as well. He had the car running and the heat on, but he couldn't really think straight and felt like he had glass shards puncturing his entire chest from the inside out.

"Married?" Bertram said out loud. He felt like all of the work he'd been doing, all of his efforts to '*adjust his expectations*', '*spend less*', get one month of take-home pay saved and now, to '*eliminate debt*' were wasted. Without Bessie, the whole thing didn't seem like it mattered much. He was stuck in a tiny apartment, not going out and enjoying himself, driving an old man's car and working ungodly hours to hit his annual numbers so that he could complete the '*Money-Strong Creed*' and live this austere life, but now that life wouldn't include Bessie. He just couldn't get his head around it.

After about fifteen minutes, he noticed his nieces were peering out at the car from bay windows in the living room and figured he'd better go in and say, "Hello". Bertram had no idea how he was going to put on a happy face when he felt so horrible inside but was resolved to give it a shot. He reached over and grabbed the housewarming gift he'd bought for Allen and Gina and the Christmas-themed stuffed animals he'd bought for the girls, bundled up, and headed in to see his brother and his family.

———

Norman tapped on Bertram's door a second time, figuring the Monday night playoff game was turned up loud enough that he didn't hear the first knock. A package had come for him over the weekend and it didn't look like Bertram had ever picked it up. Since Norman hadn't seen him in a few days he decided to bring it on up himself to deliver it before he left for the day.

He waited at the door another minute or two and headed back to the elevator, surprised that Bertram wasn't home. Norman returned the package to the locker in the lobby and headed out for the evening, hoping to bump into Bertram before he left for the holiday week on Thursday. Just in case, once he was on the freeway he asked his phone to call him, thinking he might catch him still at the office. Bertram answered but there was so much background noise Norman couldn't hear him at all and they had to sign off.

A few minutes later, Norman's phone rang and Bertram's number popped up. "Hey, Bertram, how are you my friend? Happy holidays!" Norman said, glad to finally make a connection.

"Thanks, Norman, you too… Sorry about the noise. I'm at Baxter's watching the game with some buddies," Bertram said, referring to the swanky bar and bistro down the street that was a popular hangout for professional people young enough to be Norman's children.

"Well, enjoy yourself and don't get into too much trouble," Norman ribbed his friend gently. "I seem to remember that Baxter's was a proud recipient of more than a few of your dollars in the past."

"Yeah, I'm keeping it low-key but wanted to have a little fun… Seems like I haven't done that in months," Bertram said with a drop of defensiveness seeping in.

Norman heard something in his voice that concerned him but thought better of asking about it. "Good for you, well-deserved. Just wanted to see if we'd be likely to run into each other before Thursday. We're headed up to see Irma's brother and sister for the holiday and I hoped we might connect. There's a package for you in the locker by the way... and I have a little something I was wanting to give you for Christmas as well... Maybe you could pop by tomorrow morning on your way out?"

"Sure I think that works... Depends a little on how late I get home but if not tomorrow then Wednesday morning should work fine," Bertram replied distractedly. "Hey, Norman, it's freezing out here, but when I go back in it will be crazy loud. Do you mind if I cut this a little short...? Thanks for checking on me, I'll see you tomorrow or Wednesday."

"No problem, do your thing and thanks for calling back, see you soon." Norman put his phone in his jacket pocket and wondered what was bothering Bertram. He definitely didn't sound quite right. Granted, he probably had been drinking which didn't help matters, but Norman was sensing something else too and he was saddened that he couldn't do anything to help.

He turned off the lower part of his exit ramp and drove the ten blocks to his street, not able to shake his concern, and chastising himself to 'mind his business' like his mother always used to tell him. "Sorry, mama," Norman said out loud as he pulled into the garage. "I'm still not very good at that one."

On Wednesday morning, Bertram came to see Norman at the bell stand. As usual, Norman was engaged with a tenant – one Bertram hadn't seen before – discussing holiday plans but he motioned Bertram over.

"Hi, Bertram," Norman said, gesturing towards the smartly dressed woman with a colorful holiday scarf. "This is Mrs.

Winslow from the MidRiver Bank. She's the one who helped Bessie with her mortgage issue."

Mrs. Winslow turned to Bertram, pointing a smile larger than she was in his direction and shook his hand firmly. "Very nice to meet you, Bertram!" she said with conviction.

"You as well, Mrs. Winslow," Bertram said, caught off-guard by the energy of this tiny little woman. "Bessie was so thankful for your help," he added, the mention of her name darkening him inside somewhere.

"What a lovely girl. I understand they sold the house… a prudent decision," she said with an approving tone. "I hope you'll give her my best."

Bertram shifted awkwardly. "Yes… I will do that. She will be happy to know you were thinking of her," he said deciding to be polite despite his discomfort.

"Here's my card, Bertram. If you, or someone you care about, needs assistance at the bank in the future, please feel free to reach out to me." She handed him a plain business card with blue lettering: '*Lola Winslow, Chairman and CEO.*' Bertram's eyebrows went up a bit. "Big title, small woman," Mrs. Winslow said conspiratorially.

Bertram and Norman both laughed and they all wished each other happy holidays, Mrs. Winslow giving Norman a big additional hug on the way out.

"Sorry about that, I'm sure you're trying to get to the office. How've you been, Bertram?" Norman asked once they were alone.

Bertram hesitated for a minute. "I've been good, just busy," he fibbed, not quite ready to talk about the situation with Bessie to anyone yet.

"Well, I'm glad to see you… We're heading up north tomorrow and I won't be around for a week or so. Are you going back to Weaver to see your folks for the holiday?"

Bertram nodded. "Yep, Christmas Eve at my brother

Allen's place and then Christmas Day at my parents. Should be nice…" Bertram reached into his pocket and handed his friend a very nicely wrapped, flat, rectangular box with a silver bow tied perfectly on top. "Norman, I got you a little something for Christmas."

"Wow, that's a beautiful little box, Bertram. Thank you so much." Norman handed Bertram a gift bag dotted all over with small flying reindeer and filled with red, white and green tissue.

"It's heavy!" Bertram said in surprise. "Thanks, Norman. Should we open these now?" he asked.

"Sure, let's do it," Norman said. "I'm curious what you think of my gift… and anxious to see what kind of amazing thing is inside of this beautiful box," he added, lightly shaking the package.

"You go first," Bertram suggested.

Norman carefully unwrapped the box and opened the silver lid. Under white tissue were three white Egyptian cotton handkerchiefs, emblazoned with the letters '*NP*' finely embroidered on them with a fine silver thread. Norman was visibly touched. "These are truly incredible," he said, holding one up in admiration. "I won't be letting anyone borrow one of these anytime soon." He gave Bertram a big hug. "Thank you, my friend, very thoughtful of you."

"I thought you might need a few extras," Bertram said with a sly grin, fishing inside the bag Norman gave him and pulling out a canvas bag that was fairly heavy duty and zipped up at the top.

"Look inside," Norman coaxed.

In the bag was everything someone could possibly need for a spring picnic including a finely made blanket, plates and bowls of hard plastic and even wine glasses made of stainless steel Thermos material that still managed to look elegant without stems.

"Man, this is awesome," Bertram said, trying hard not to think about Bessie. "Can't wait until the thaw so I can use it. Thanks, Norman!" He put the canvas bag down and gave his friend a big hug. "You've been a huge help to me, Norman. Thank you again for everything."

They were saying goodbye when Norman remembered the package Bertram had received, retrieving it from the locker and handing it to him.

"I guess I'll go run these upstairs," Bertram said, checking his watch and taking the package from Norman. "Have a great holiday, Norman, and please give my love to Irma."

Norman nodded. "Will do, and you to Bessie," he responded.

Bertram assured him that he would, finding it too difficult to explain his situation for now. "I'll call you between Christmas and New Year at some point," he promised and hopped into the elevator.

Bertram was seated at the bar and waiting on Simon. Simon's wife was just over eight months' pregnant with their first child and Bertram hadn't seen much of him for a while as they were busy trying to get their place set up for a newborn among other things. He was absently watching sports news on the set behind the bar when he felt a hand on his shoulder.

"Hey, man, how've you been?" the hand's owner asked. Lance Garner was a friend from college and a fellow football player whom Bertram saw a few times a year, mostly at big parties.

Lance had been to law school right after college and had

recently joined a big firm in the city. He was a lot of fun and someone that Bertram enjoyed hanging out with. They gave each other a big hug and Lance introduced his date, a very beautiful and slightly intoxicated woman Bertram hadn't seen before. They exchanged small talk for a moment and the server came over to let Lance know his table was ready. Lance and Bertram said their goodbyes with promises to get together in the new year and Lance and his date started walking off towards their table.

Lance stopped as he was just exiting the bar area and motioned his date to follow the server, doubling back for a second. "Oh, hey, Bertram, I didn't want to say anything in front of Kristen because she's not invited but… a couple of us big-leaguers are going to the Super Bowl and I wondered if you wanted to join us? It's in Miami so it will be epic, and warm!" They both laughed.

Bertram took a deep breath. "How much are the tickets?" he asked, knowing he shouldn't be considering it – he had just started paying down his debt and was making pretty good progress.

"Face value is four thousand five hundred dollars but we got a discount since I bought a package so you'd only pay three thousand five hundred. You in?"

Bertram thought for a moment. It would set him back almost two full months of debt-elimination just for the ticket, not to mention the airfare, hotel and all of the expensive debauchery they would certainly get up to. He knew there was no way it was a good idea. "Yes, that sounds awesome. I'm in," Bertram replied, without thinking.

"Awesome, I'll have Liz, my paralegal, send you the ticket and you can get me the money whenever."

Bertram gave his friend a handshake and turned back to the bar, noticing that Simon had texted:

"*Super-late, sorry man. Can we do it another time?*"

Bertram was a little annoyed that his friend would text to cancel a few minutes after they were going to meet. "That's fine, let's catch up in January," he shot back.

"Miss you, dude. Things are crazy right now…" Simon replied, obviously feeling bad.

"No worries. Have a good holiday," Bertram responded.

Bertram sat at the bar nursing his beer, watching sports news and feeling lonely and at odds with himself. "What's the point of being '*Money-Strong*' if I can't live a little," he thought, trying to justify the extravagant Super Bowl decision. "The whole thing seems sort of pointless."

He ordered some food from the bartender and contemplated things for a while before noticing the two women sitting next to him and striking up a conversation,

The weather continued to be punishingly cold, making the first two weeks of the new year particularly grueling. Getting back into the swing of things after the holidays proved difficult in the best of circumstances, but the added complication of snow, ice and frigid temperatures put the brakes on most activity, including getting client activity in motion.

The office was fairly quiet as Bertram set up for his day, most people opting to avoid the weather and to work from home. He was disappointed with his year end, having made a last push with his team to hit the thirty-five percent growth number Mr. Vaughan had established for his region. They had fallen short, meaning that he didn't hit the highest bonus tier and also fell just shy of qualifying for President's Club. More importantly, Vaughan had set his goal for the new year at thirty-five percent growth again which felt completely impossible, especially given that he was losing one of his best people who had just been promoted to Bertram's position in another market. Bertram sighed and sifted back through his client and prospect list, trying to figure out where that extra growth was going to come from and feeling more than a little defeated.

His phone buzzed him back to earth. "Hey, Norman," Bertram answered after a moment looking at the number.

"Hi, Bertram, how was your holiday…? I've only seen the back of your head a couple of times since I've been back," Norman kidded him.

"Yeah, sorry I've not had a chance to come down and chat. The last week has been crazy," Bertram explained only half truthfully since he was also avoiding the need to share Bessie's news and his trip to the Super Bowl. "My holiday was great, it's really nice having Allen back in the area and spending time with him and his family. How was your trip?" Bertram was happy to move the attention elsewhere.

"Trip was good, trip was good. A little too much dangerously good cooking for this big guy if I'm being honest," Norman said laughing, "I'm not so good at throttling it back when the food is so fine and Irma wasn't too happy with me straying from my diet." Norman's doctor had scolded him for letting his blood pressure get too high and was determined to help him keep it down without medication since Norman's fitness level was solid and he took good care of himself in all other ways.

Bertram chuckled and shook his head. "I would never stop eating if I lived with that wife of yours," he admitted.

"Just imagine what it's like when you've got two more of them in the house," Norman responded, meaning Irma's two sisters, "It's like a factory of all things delicious."

They caught up a bit, chatting pleasantly, Bertram feeling

himself relax as he talked to his friend. Shortly before they were about to hang up, Norman got to why he was calling.

"Speaking of great food, I wanted to invite you to watch the Super Bowl with us this year. We always do an incredible spread with burgers Donald hand-grinds out of three kinds of meat, and some of Irma's special potatoes that I swear are so good they should be illegal. Since you can't have too big a bash at your place this year, I thought you might like to join us."

"I'm surprised Irma lets you eat those burgers at all," Bertram pointed out, thinking about Norman's blood pressure.

"Well, she only lets me have one. If I'm lucky, I get one the next day in my lunch as leftovers too," Norman shared conspiratorially. "She watches me like a hawk."

Bertram was thankful for the invitation but was squirming for a response. He didn't want to share the Super Bowl trip with Norman, fearing that he'd be judged or get a lecture or both. He also wasn't really ready for the conversation with Norman about Bessie. "That's a really tempting offer," he said, not sure of what else he was going to say, "but I'm thinking about doing something smaller at my place with a few friends. Haven't quite figured it out yet. Can I get back to you in a couple of days?" Bertram kicked the can down the road, feeling like stalling would give him just enough time to figure out how he was going to talk to Norman about things.

"Sure, Bertram, no problem. Just let me know by next Wednesday," he said pleasantly. "Oh, I almost forgot… Irma invited Bessie as well, hope that was ok. She stopped by to give back that old handkerchief when we got back from the holiday and they were chatting… She sounded like she was going to make it.".

Bertram felt his heart sink, wondering if she shared her news about her engagement to Tom. "Oh, that's… great, yes, thanks for doing that." He tried to play it cool to see what

Norman might mention.

"She's a great young lady… Anyway, just let me know in a couple of days…" Norman responded and they signed off.

Bertram unlocked and opened the top drawer of his desk and looked at the envelope that held his Super Bowl ticket. He took it out for a moment before sliding it back in and relocking the drawer, pausing a moment before attempting to drag his attention back to his work.

– – –

This time, Simon was waiting for Bertram at the restaurant when Bertram arrived. They hadn't managed to get together before the holidays and Bertram was happy to see his old friend. After they gave each other a hug and said a brief "Hello", Simon pointed to the counter and suggested that they order. He looked tired and a little disheveled, having barely recovered from the chaos of bringing an infant into the world.

Bertram had planned on going to the hospital to visit but the baby came a couple of weeks early and there had been a few complications. Fortunately, they were able to bring their little girl home last week and mom, dad and baby seemed to be doing well, other than in the sleeping department.

"Well, I guess this is your life now," Bertram said as they walked to the counter to order. "No more of our sloppy boy's nights at one of our favorite steakhouses," Bertram kidded, having originally suggested the same place where they failed to connect in December.

"Yeah, pretty much anything that takes more than about forty-five minutes is off the table if I'm going to stay married right now. Plus, I'm trying to be sympathetic to the fact that Melinda can't drink alcohol while she's breastfeeding, so resisting temptation is a good plan."

It had been a big year for Simon who had gotten married and had a baby all within about an eleven-month span. Simon shook his head. "From martinis and porterhouses to diapers and egg *foo yung*, it seems like a bit of a tailspin doesn't it?" he lamented with a sheepish grin, grabbing utensils and napkins from a series of bins under the *'please bus your own table'* sign next to the trash cans.

Bertram went up to retrieve their food when the cashier called their number and plopped down across from his friend. "So what's it like?" he asked with genuine interest.

"What, you mean fatherhood? Or marriage?" Simon tried to clarify.

Bertram laughed. "Both."

"Well, I have to say, even with the lack of sleep and all of the whirlwind of activity, it's…" Simon searched for the right words…"incredible."

Bertram furrowed his brow. "How so?"

"That little tiny life… completely reliant upon you for everything. It really alters your perspective. Plus, you fall in love with a baby in a way I just couldn't fathom when fathers or mothers would subject me to pictures of their kids in the past. Now I'm probably just as idiotic as they were." Bertram nodded while he ate a potsticker. "And Melinda has been such a trooper. We both got battle-tested during the birth process and it was super scary… Melinda was like a buddha. She ended up having to reassure me the whole time and was still able to find the energy to breastfeed and put on a sunny face for the few visitors that were allowed in. It really was touch and go for the first week… and all of that after her being in and out of labor for almost thirty-six hours." Simon took a deep breath. "It was a lot. She's amazing and I feel so lucky."

Bertram and Simon sat in silence, soaking in the power of Simon's emotions and savoring their meals.

"Man, this is a good place, you're lucky to have it so close by…" Simon said, reading Bertram's mind.

"Yeah, it is awesome… I… come here often," Bertram said flashing on the memory of his chance meeting with Bessie and their dinner here.

He and Simon caught up on people they had in common for a while before returning to more personal matters. "So are you having your Super Bowl party this year?" Simon asked. "Maybe a little group of the hardcore OGs?"

Bertram shook his head. "Nah," he said, pausing to consider what he wanted to share. "I was actually thinking of going to the game," he blurted as if admitting to a crime.

"To the game?" Simon looked as shocked as he felt. "Aren't those tickets like thousands of dollars?"

"Well, yeah, but do you remember Lance from college?" Simon nodded. "He got a group rate so I decided what the heck, I deserve a break and I've never been… Why not?"

Simon considered this for a moment, digesting it. "But, I thought you were working hard to get in a… different financial spot, and that was going really well, wasn't it? Wouldn't this derail you a little?" Simon didn't look directly at his friend, hoping not to offend him.

"No, it's actually just a little speed bump. I can get back to it without much impact," Bertram replied, not entirely truthfully since he knew he'd be extending his ability to '*eliminate debt*' by at least four months once he included all of the trip expenses.

Simon shrugged and didn't respond, content to leave it at that. "Sounds like fun," he said, "and something I won't even get to think about for many years…"

Bertram stayed fairly quiet, asking Simon some more questions about life with a newborn and finishing dinner. They gave each other a warm hug before stepping out of the Chinese restaurant into the frigid air, coming up with a date that Bertram could come by the house and see Melinda and meet the new addition before parting ways.

It was snowing again, on Super Bowl Sunday, but it had lightened to flurries by the time that Bessie rang the doorbell at the Price residence. Bessie was mummified in layers and Irma helped her unwind herself from the various coats, scarves and sweaters that she had layered on, both of them giggling at the process.

Norman, Donald, and Donald's brother, Reggie, were already watching the pregame but all came out to properly say, "Hello" to Bessie before returning stealthily to the den to absorb themselves in the game.

Irma introduced Bessie to Donald's wife Margo and Reggie's girlfriend Sondra who greeted her kindly before turning back to their assigned jobs as *sous* chefs. Margo was using a mandoline to slice wafer-thin onions and Sondra was cutting potatoes into perfect, half-inch squares, while Irma was whipping up something in the food processor. Periodically, one of the women would bring something over to Irma to inspect and she would offer a suggestion or comment, sending them off to return to their station.

Bessie, feeling weird to be standing there leaning against the counter while everyone else was knee-deep in work asked if she could help.

Irma chuckled. "Careful what you wish for," she said, pulling a roll of dough wrapped in cellophane from the refrigerator. "Have you ever rolled out a pie crust?"

"Yes, but not often. My grandmother on my father's side was a fabulous baker but she didn't trust me if the stakes were high," Bessie shared honestly.

Irma nodded with a smile. "Well, let's see if you make the

grade," she said, handing Bessie the pan, the ball of dough, and clearing a spot for her to work. The pan had fluted edges which would make it a little easier for Bessie to get the look right. "There's no top... We're making pecan pie so if you can roll it nice and thin and trim the excess, that's all there is to it. I'm working on the filling now... Happy to check the progress or stay out of your hair," Irma said, already headed back to her spot in the kitchen.

The ladies bantered and joked while they worked, laughing as much as they were cooking. Bessie fell into the easy rhythm of the work and the comfortable nature of their conversation, shocked when Donald came in to share that it was almost halftime.

"Tradition is, the gentlemen cook up the burgers at halftime so we can watch the performances, then we all eat in the den while the game finishes up," Irma explained to Bessie.

Donald checked on their baby who had been down for a nap and came back to the kitchen holding a big smiling package of cuteness. After appropriate attention from his adoring fans, baby and mom disappeared for a feeding and Donald went to retrieve the men for their assigned cooking duties.

After dinner, and the best desserts that Bessie had ever eaten in her life, Irma and Bessie found themselves quietly scraping the last of a pile of dishes together to prepare them for the dishwasher. Like earlier in the day, they fell into a peaceful motion that felt more like dancing than cleaning dirty plates.

"I've been wanting to ask you," Irma said, speaking softly so as not to break their flow. "How did Bertram react to your engagement?"

Bessie had shared the news with the table at dessert, the big game having come to a close, getting genuine well-wishes and congratulations all around. She looked for, but couldn't observe, a hint of surprise from Irma or Norman, not being able to tell if they already knew. They were extremely gracious and overtly supportive, putting her at ease and making her wonder if it wouldn't have been such a bad idea to have brought Tom after all. Even though Irma had told her that Bertram wasn't coming, she thought bringing Tom over was a little presumptuous, especially knowing their relationship with Bertram.

"I... I'm not entirely sure," she answered honestly. "I haven't talked to him much since Tom and I told him before Christmas. But it seems pretty clear by his distance that he's hurt by it."

Irma nodded, bringing over the last of the coffee cups and saucers from the table. "I think he has it for you something fierce," she said smiling. "It's not the kind of wound that heals quickly."

"I really... I like Bertram so much. When we were kids, I was completely in love with him," Bessie replied with some pain in her voice. "I don't want to hurt him. I just don't... I can't see how we can be together. We're so different... and I feel those differences will be impossible to get past. He's..." Bessie trailed off, shaking her head. She had stopped cleaning dishes and was leaning against the sink, looking out the bay window that framed the white flurries reflecting back at her as they fell in the Price's backyard.

"Bertram has been sharing with Norman some of the things he was working to change... and I have a pretty good feeling that he was doing a lot of that in hopes you might feel differently." Irma gently nudged Bessie out of the way, rubbing her on the arm lightly in order to finish cleaning the cups that stood in a pile where Bessie had given up her post.

Bessie cocked her head in curiosity. "Bertram was... working with Norman. What do you mean by that?" she asked. Bessie had a vague recollection that Bertram had mentioned Norman's influence when they were over last time, most vividly remembering the plaque he showed her that contained the '*Money-Strong Creed*'.

Irma dried her hands with a fluffy kitchen towel with an embroidered rooster on it, folding it neatly and hanging it on the sink. "Norman learned a lot about managing his finances from my father. He worked for him for many years while he was trying to make something of himself. Truth is, I think he was more concerned with making eyes at me than he was much of anything for a long time. Anyway, my father passed on some of his wisdom to Norman and Norman has been doing the same for others – when they ask or seek him out. He doesn't see himself as a preacher spreading the gospel, only as a friend." Irma motioned Bessie to a couple of the barstools at the counter where they sat down with two glasses of iced water.

"So… Bertram asked Norman for help?" Bessie asked quizzically. "That doesn't really sound like Bertram," she added with a raise of her eyebrows.

Irma laughed. "Well, he did have some pretty big motivation I think," she said, looking at Bessie with amusement. "Anyway, Norman shared something called the '*Money-Strong Creed*' with him – something my father learned from his own mentor in business. It's just a simple way to live a life free from money anxiety and in control of your financial world. Bertram was doing a really good job at getting things in order from what I understand," Irma said matter-of-factly.

Bessie registered a little surprise. "And he's stuck with it? I… That's just so far from what I know about Bertram. I mean, he always wanted fancy things and a bigger life. He didn't ever really seem to me like he could… or wanted to… change that. I don't… I need someone super-stable in my life. He has always seemed a little dangerous. I can't…" Bessie just shook her head.

Irma looked at Bessie and took her hands. "Bessie, if you

love someone, sometimes you have to take a chance. Look at the knucklehead I married," she joked. Irma patted Bessie's hands softly. "All I can say is that there are some risks worth taking… especially when you know your own heart."

"But I really love Tom… I think we're a good match," Bessie said defensively. "He and I have a lot in common and we have a lot of fun together," she added as if she were pleading her case.

Irma, put her hand on Bessie's cheek. "I'm sure you do, baby," she said. "But loving someone is different than being in love with them." Irma got up as a way to change the subject, leaving Bessie alone to contemplate their conversation while she helped Donald and Margo get the baby's stuff together and get bundled up to hit the road.

"Hi, Norman," Bertram said, waving to his friend as he entered the lobby from the street.

"Whoa, man, you look like you just stepped off of a beach somewhere," Norman said, pretending to look startled. "Where the heck you been? I know for sure you didn't get that color hanging around here." Norman angled his head toward the gray, slush-filled streets, illuminated by the early evening streetlamps.

Bertram laughed. "No, no I've been on a trip for the weekend. Kind of wanted to talk to you, actually. Do you have time to catch up?" Bertram was finally ready to come clean about everything that had been going on in his life.

"Sure, I can always make time for you, my friend." Norman looked at his watch. "How about you pop down around six-thirty before I head out? I told Irma I'd be home by seven-thirty but we could chat for a half hour or so?"

Bertram nodded. "Sounds good. Why don't you just come up to the apartment when you're ready? I'll pour you a cup of tea… I've still got some of that weird peppermint stuff you like laying around, I think." Norman gave him an enthusiastic thumbs up.

Bertram had barely had a chance to change out of his work clothes when his doorbell rang and he scampered over to let Norman in.

"Sorry, you busy?" Norman asked. "I got Archie to cover since I thought it would be nice to get a little more time together, but I can come back…" Norman paused at the threshold rather than going in.

"No, no," Bertram held the door open and ushered his friend in, "I'm glad you're early." They sat down on the sofa, which Norman gave an approving little bounce on after getting situated.

"You've made this place really nice, Bertram," he said, appraising the rest of the apartment. "You have some good taste, don't you?"

"Thanks, Norman," Bertram said, looking a bit embarrassed. "The lighting really helps… Since the building blocks a lot of the natural light I worked to make it feel a little bigger than the sardine can it actually is."

"Good for you," Norman said, waiting patiently to see if his friend was going to explain his movie-star tan or if he'd have to ask him about it directly.

Bertram cleared his throat. "Norman, I…" He paused to consider how to say it. "I've been struggling," he finally blurted. Norman's eyebrows shot up, encouraging him to continue. "I didn't come this weekend, not because I was having a Super Bowl party, but because I actually went to the Super Bowl…" Bertram stopped to gauge Norman's reaction, which was non-existent… "which isn't the whole story. I also couldn't bring myself to face Bessie… She's, well, she's getting married, and honestly, I wasn't ready to talk to anyone about it. I've never… I've never felt like this before… I thought that going to the Super Bowl and partying with friends would make it better. I thought avoiding it and thinking about other things, going out with a few girls, would be distracting and take my mind off of it. But no, I still feel like garbage." Bertram hung his head a little, rubbing the side of his face, obviously in pain. Norman didn't respond but put his hand on Bertram's shoulder.

After a few minutes, Bertram opened up like an oil gusher and shared the whole story: how he had decided to blow his entire debt elimination plan for a few days of fun; how he thought that would feel better but actually felt worse; how he didn't know what end was up. "The crazy thing is," he said, "when I got to Miami on Friday night, I didn't even feel like partying with everyone else. I ended up nursing a few whiskies at the bar while everyone else did the things I used to instigate until some ungodly hour. By the morning, I had decided I was going to sell my ticket and go back home. Strangely, one of the guys I had been chatting with a little at the bar was seated next to me at breakfast the next day and I happened to mention that I had a ticket to sell.

"Twenty minutes later, I had almost recovered all of the ticket money and was headed to the airport. Turned out, all the flights were booked until the next day and since my heart wasn't into the scene, I found a quiet, cheap beachfront hotel in Fort Lauderdale and spent Saturday thinking about things." Bertram looked over at Norman. "Sorry, do you need an intermission?" he joked. "I'm only about halfway through." Norman smiled and shook his head but didn't speak, hesitant to interrupt Bertram's flow.

"Ok cool, so I was thinking all day. About Bessie.

About being '*Money-Strong*'. I felt horrible about losing the opportunity to spend my life with Bessie, but I felt almost as bad about betraying myself." Bertram stopped for a second and took a sip of the tea he had forgotten about. "I guess I had figured that me working on getting '*Money-Strong*' was about me trying to get Bessie to give me a chance, and maybe it was. But, then, I don't know. Now I'm feeling like I needed to get '*Money-Strong*' for me too. The lifestyle I was living used to be so much fun – I didn't think about how much I spent and just did what I wanted... It was free and easy and I genuinely loved it. Somehow the whole thing has just started seeming empty and lonely, like everything flipped on its head. It felt way better to take the money from the Super Bowl ticket I had sold to keep myself on the path to debt elimination than to hang with friends and spend a bunch of money I didn't really have. Anyway, I'm still not sure what to do about Bessie, but I know I want to keep on the '*Money-Strong*' path." Bertram had been holding his mug and put it back on the coffee table. "So, I guess that's the story," he said, spreading his hands wide to underscore the width of it.

"Wow, my friend, that's a lot to take in," Norman said compassionately. "Quite a journey you've been on for the last few weeks. I'm sure it was hard to decide to sell that ticket... especially after you'd travelled all that way. I also think that you have made a big leap that you haven't recognized since whatever happens with Bessie, you've put yourself on a path that will bring you a much richer life. You will have choices you wouldn't have ever had before and you'll be able to do things that most people can't, just because you've put yourself in a position where your appetites and your desire for short-term pleasure aren't driving your decisions." Norman nodded. "That's a really admirable thing Bertram."

"Thanks, Norman," Bertram said, relieved that Norman didn't express disappointment over a few of the choices he had made and feeling supported by his friend. "It's been a heck of a rocky ride lately," he admitted, running a hand through his hair.

"Let me tell you a quick story," Norman said. "You remember how I shared that Mr. Sykes wouldn't let me date Irma until I had gotten my… stuff… together with the '*Money-Strong Creed*'?" Bertram nodded. "Well, that's only half of that part of the story. You see, once I had gotten that worked out to his satisfaction, I still had to convince Irma that A) I existed and B) I was worthy of more than two seconds of her attention." Norman folded his arms behind his head. "And boy, that girl wanted none of that at all!" Norman laughed at the memory.

"So what did you do?" Bertram asked. Norman shook his head and leaned forward. "Man, I'll tell you, I did every stupid thing I could think of. I had a friend of mine play guitar while I tried to serenade her with a Marvin Gaye tune – keep in mind I'm as tone deaf as a stump, so that probably wasn't one of my better ideas. I found out where she got her hair done and had roses delivered while she was there so all the women would "*ooh*" and "*aah*". I even borrowed a limo from my uncle who had an airport limousine service to pick her up at church one day. Not a single one of those made any impact.

"One day, after about a year of these shenanigans, I was at church loading chairs back into the rectory storage room. There had been an Easter event and quite a few extra parishioners had come out for it, so there must've been a hundred or so chairs out there. Mr. Sykes was a church deacon and had asked me for help with the chairs… I suggested that he go on home and I'd take care of it, not knowing that there wouldn't be anyone else to help.

"Truth was, I didn't really mind. I liked doing hard work, especially for people I cared about, and it seemed that there weren't that many other folks in the kind of shape to haul all that around so it wasn't a big deal. As I was loading the last stack in and locking up the room, I turned around to leave and almost bumped straight into Irma. Now keep in mind, I must've looked like something from a horror movie, my church clothes soaked through with sweat and all scuffed up from the dirty chairs. But she just looked at me and smiled." Norman stopped talking as if that was the end of the story.

"Ok, but then what happened?" Bertram said. "That can't be the end of the story??" He looked as if he'd waited overnight in line for a big movie opening and the people behind him started arguing loudly just before the big fight scene at the end between the hero and the villain.

Norman took a second, irritating Bertram, before he started back up. "Well, I said hello to her, not quite in my right mind, and she told me to come to the Sykes' house for dinner that night. I wasn't sure whether she was a messenger for her father or whether she was asking me herself, but either way, I couldn't say yes fast enough.

"We talked for hours after that dinner and she said something to me while I reluctantly took notice of the time, wanting to respect her parents and leave at a decent hour. What Irma said was, "All that fluff doesn't impress me... I want to know what kind of man you are – that's what matters". I wonder what would have happened if she hadn't had choir practice that afternoon, or if the practice room didn't have a window facing the church lawn. Would she have seen what kind of man I was? Would she have known I was the kind of man who would happily work to make life easier for the people I loved?"

Bertram looked at Norman, clearly moved by the story. "I'm sure glad you didn't have to find out," Bertram said after a time.

"You and me both," Norman concurred with a grin.

It felt good to Bertram to be back on track with his '*Money-Strong*' plan and to have shared his whole story with Norman, warts and all. He wasn't used to speaking with that kind of honesty when he was talking about his personal life and something about it was liberating, as if the tiny half-truths and intentional omissions built an internal igloo, block-by-block, that froze his heart, and that the truth somehow heated it all back up again.

He had an amazing visit with Simon and Melinda, holding their baby for almost an hour while it slept. It seemed odd to him that he enjoyed cradling that little softly breathing lump in his hands for so long, especially since he had never had much interest in kids, something he figured might change as he got older but never had thought much about. He was also surprised by how comfortable it was to hang with Simon and Melinda in their tiny little cottage. It was barely big enough for a legitimate kitchen table but they had fixed it up beautifully and made it feel both welcoming and special, reminding him of how hard it had been to make the studio palatable after living in such a lavish apartment.

Bertram tried to shake a twinge of sadness that gripped him when he thought that this could have been the life he would have created with Bessie if the world were a different place. Fortunately, his melancholy was moderated by the sheer joy that his friend and Melinda were experiencing and his own genuine pleasure and gratitude for their happiness.

Some unseasonably warm March weather found Bertram in his car, headed towards Weaver. He had promised Allen that he would help him rebuild the back fence and figured they might as well get it over with. Although the ground was still too frozen to dig out and replace any of the post holes, they could redo the portion that still had sturdy newer redwood posts.

He looked forward to spending time with Allen since their age difference made it almost as if they were getting to know each other for the first time. In many ways, Allen was more like his father than his brother, even with his easy-going nature and wry sense of humor matching the cadence of their father's. While Allen had a good job as an accountant at the largest factory in town, he was incredibly handy and could build or rebuild darn near anything, something he also was handed down from his father but perfected during the many years he worked as a junior millwright while putting himself through school. He didn't need much airtime, but when he spoke, it was with clarity and consideration, making him a reliable source of advice and a good compliment to Bertram who both required more words and appreciated his brother's counsel.

Bertram sat chatting with Gina on the back porch while Allen finished doing something with the girls upstairs. The weather was warm enough that they both felt comfortable in light jackets and sweaters, which was almost like sitting around in a swimsuit compared to how things had been lately.

Allen came around the side of the house carrying redwood fencing slats, Bertram's cue to wrap things up and get to work. He gave the girls a quick hug – they had both made their way outside in search of their mother – and wandered to the fenceline to help Allen get started. Allen nodded at him and gave him a shoulder pat, motioning him back to the pile of fencing materials on the side yard. Bertram walked behind his brother, noticing a very slight right-side limp and asked about it, but Allen waved it off as nothing without having to say a word, grabbing another stack of wood while Bertram handled the other side.

They continued working together in relative silence for quite some time before Bertram spoke up.

"How's everyone adjusting?" he asked, wondering how it felt for them to leave New Jersey after so many years.

Allen shrugged. "Kids seem to be doing well... Gina has reconnected with some old friends. It's been good," he said, motioning to Bertram to help him level the fence slats.

"How are you doing?" Allen asked with sincere interest.

"I'm... good. I mean, yeah, I'm good," Bertram wasn't sure how much his brother wanted to hear or how much he wanted to share. After a few minutes though, Bertram just started to talk. He told Allen about Norman and his financial goals, the situation with Bessie, and even the trip to Miami. It seemed natural and with the exception of a very periodic question, Allen just listened in between an instruction or redirection.

At some point, Gina hollered at them from the back deck to come and grab some lunch, having laid out some sandwiches and drinks for them on the big built-in deck table. Bertram shouted his thanks and after finishing installing a few more boards, they wandered up to eat.

"Man, I'm starving," Bertram acknowledged. "I can't believe it's already two-thirty."

Allen nodded as he picked up a sandwich and ate. Bertram looked a little more closely at his brother while they ate lunch, thinking that he looked a little thinner than when he'd seen him last.

"How much more do you have time for?" Allen said, motioning towards the fence with his head after methodically polishing off two sandwiches and refilling his water bottle.

Bertram shrugged. "I'm happy to help you until about four, if that's cool," he answered, not wanting to disappoint his brother.

"Sure, that'd be great." Allen unfolded his lanky body and

headed back down to the work site, leaving Bertram to shove the last few bites of a sandwich into his mouth before heading down to join him.

"Allen, you mind if I ask you question?" Bertram said between short bursts from the cordless drill. Allen made a face that invited him to continue. "What would you do about Bessie? I feel like I should really make one last effort... tell her how I feel and see if it works. But then again, I want to do what's right for her... and I don't want to screw up her life. She seems to like Tom well enough and who am I to get in the way...?" Bertram didn't quite finish the thought. Allen didn't respond for a long enough period of time to cause Bertram to wonder if he had heard him.

"Do you love her?" Allen asked, two wood screws sticking out of his mouth.

"I do," Bertram answered without hesitation.

"Well, then you need to tell her that and ask her if there's some way she might love you too," Allen said. "I'm not really sure you've ever had that conversation with her, have you?"

Bertram considered that for a moment, reflecting back on their conversations. "No, it was probably more indirect than that," he admitted.

Allen shrugged. "Probably worth the time," he said with understated calm.

"How does it feel?" Bertram asked. "Being married, having a family, kids... Is it... fun?"

Allen looked at him with a smile. "All of the time? Definitely not. But it's better than that... It just matters a lot. Different from other things in your life. Not every day is great or even good and all that somehow makes you a better man. A better person." Allen shrugged. "That'll about do it for the day," he said in resignation to the evening dusk already crawling in. "I'm going to put this stuff away; you're welcome to go in and clean up instead."

"No, let me help you with this," Bertram said, and together they stood back for a minute, admiring their accomplishment before tidying up and heading on in.

It was a little after five-thirty by the time Bertram was back in his car, later than he had expected. Impulsively, he called Bessie but she didn't pick up. He fought the impulse to hang up and instead left a voicemail, asking her to call him back. On a whim, he called his parents, figuring it might be good to swing by and say, "Hello" while he was in town. He got his mom who was in the midst of cooking dinner and she invited him by. He usually would have passed on the last-minute invitation but decided to take her up on it, feeling bad that he didn't even mention he'd be around Weaver.

Bertram gave his mom and dad a hug and went into the kitchen to chat with his mother for a while as she finished dinner, helping her set the table at the same time. They mostly made small talk and caught up on things, not having seen each other for over a month.

Bertram's mom seemed a little out of sorts which was very unusual – she always was kind and attentive, making you feel like the only person in the room as a matter of pride.

"What's wrong, Mom, something on your mind?" Bertram asked when the appropriate moment presented itself.

She hesitated for a moment and it took Bertram a second to realize that she was crying. This alarmed him… He couldn't even remember seeing his mom cry other than one time when her own mother had died many years ago. Bertram wrapped her up in his arms, just trying to comfort her while resisting the urge to ask what was wrong. She pulled away after a moment and found a Kleenex, composed herself and took a deep breath.

"Mom, what is going on?" Bertram finally asked after waiting what seemed like forever. She stood facing the sink with her hands propped on the sides.

"You were at Allen's for a bit today?" she started, Bertram's heart rapidly sinking into his feet.

"Yes," he managed, scared about what was coming.

"You probably noticed that he'd lost some weight," she said, "not that he had a lot to lose." Allen was always strong and wiry, built more like Bertram's father's side of the family – taller and thinner than his mother's stock. Bertram nodded in agreement. His mom sighed. "He has leukemia… and it's pretty advanced. I thought he would tell you… but you know how he is."

Bertram sat in the closest chair, the blood rushing from his head. "What, I mean, I don't…" Bertram couldn't process what she was saying. They'd worked all day long and Allen more than kept up… He'd actually led the pace. "How… When did you find out?"

"A few weeks ago, but he and Gina had been keeping it to themselves for a while. Apparently, they wanted to have a treatment plan before they told anyone… and they still haven't told the kids," she said.

Bertram held his head in his hands. He felt the familiar anger building up inside of him: anger at the world, anger at his brother, anger at himself for not seeing signs that seemed obvious in retrospect. He took a few deep breaths to lower his boiling point and let his mom tell him what she knew. The bottom line was, his brother was very sick and Bertram wasn't sure there was anything he could do about it.

Bertram opted to stay at his parents that night, not being up for the drive home after finishing dinner. He took a long shower and went right to bed, his physical exhaustion helping him to sleep soundly despite the trauma of the evening's news.

He woke early and thinking about Allen, trying to decide how to bring up his illness with him, opting to stay in bed so he wouldn't wake his parents. He distracted himself by reading some news on his phone when a text message buzzed in from Bessie:

"*Sorry I missed you… Call me sometime today before 11am if you have time and we can catch up.*"

Even though the message wasn't much, it still made him feel better just having it. He texted her back, saying that he'd call her around nine. He found a pair of jeans and a t-shirt in his drawer that still fit pretty well, took another quick shower and spent a little time with his parents, opting to call Bessie somewhere outside in order to have some privacy. Bertram still had no idea what he was going to do about talking to Allen, but the wound was so fresh that he wasn't sure he was ready for that conversation anyway.

The day was almost as pleasant as the previous one and he drove up to the square to call Bessie from one of the benches with a nice view of town hall.

"Hello, Bertram," Bessie answered.

Bertram felt some of the stress he'd been holding in his chest lighten. "Hi, Bess," he said, trying not to sound as sad and messed up as he felt.

"You ok?" she asked, immediately sensing that something was wrong.

"I… honestly, not really," he admitted, feeling the sadness over his brother in the pit of his stomach.

"Where are you?" she asked, her voice strong with protective concern.

"Believe it or not, I'm sitting in the plaza on a bench," he said.

"You mean, in Weaver?" she asked, confused.

"Yeah, I stayed at my folks last night…" he said. "Don't worry, they're fine," he assured her, knowing that would be the next question. Bessie loved Bertram's parents and felt almost as close to his mother as her own.

"Do you want me to come down there?" she asked. "I don't have anything going on until eleven-thirty, so…"

"I mean, yeah, that would be really great," he said with mixed feelings, not sure he could hold it together for her right now but not wanting to be without her either. "

See you in ten," she said and was gone before he could tell her what side of the square he was parked on.

He saw Bessie's old sedan pull in behind the Hyundai and watched her as she exited the car and walked with purpose towards him. The light was at her back and she was wearing a sundress with a denim jacket, making her look like some kind of indie movie star with a magical aura as her superpower. He was so captivated by her, Bertram forgot his problems for a few seconds.

When she reached him, he tried to snap himself back to reality, giving her a hug and thanking her for coming while feeling a little guilty that she had to interrupt her Sunday to 'fix' him.

"It's good to see you, Bertram, I missed you at the Price's Super Bowl party," she said in a way that put him further at ease, giving him a hug before sitting next to him and turning so that they were almost facing each other.

"Thanks, yeah, I... That's a bit of a story, actually..." he laughed at himself.

Bessie looked at him quizzically but didn't press him. "Sounds interesting," she said lightly without judgment. "So... what's going on, Bertram? I can see that something isn't right... Do you want to talk about it?"

Bertram looked back at her, not realizing that tears had started to stream down his face, causing her to tear up as well.

"Oh my gosh, what's happening?" Bessie asked. "I've literally never seen you cry in all of the years we've known each other, not even when we were tiny," she said, overwhelmed.

"Allen is really sick," was all Bertram could manage.

They held each other for a while before Bertram was able

to pull himself together and tell her as much as he knew. She held his hand for a while and then he walked her to her car, knowing that she had to get back to her life.

"I'm really glad we could see each other," Bertram said. "Thank you for coming out. You didn't have to…" he said with appreciation.

"Of course I did," she said sternly. "We're practically family, Bertram."

He nodded, not sure what else to say at that moment, and they said their goodbyes with Bertram promising to keep her in the loop. As Bertram sat in his car for a moment, he felt powerless over so many things in his life. But he also was clear on one thing, he wanted so much to live his life with the girl with the kind heart and the magical aura that he wanted to deserve her love.

Bertram had called Norman on the drive back to the city and shared with him what was happening, not wanting the tortured companionship of his own thoughts. Norman listened and offered his support, but mostly Bertram was just happy to have a friend who had his best interests in mind and was willing to let him vent his feelings without judgment.

He was beginning to realize the same things he appreciated about Norman were some of the things he loved about Bessie and it surprised him a little that he didn't seem to notice or value those things as much in his life before. In many ways, Bertram was finding life to be more complicated and confusing but somehow more meaningful at the same time.

The work week was a blur, Bertram trying to stay focused

on helping his team to hit their first-quarter objective so that the region could have a shot at the annual growth target. It felt good to have the distraction of work and although he couldn't get Allen out of his thoughts, he put his energy and focus into the deals that were necessary to get him and his people to the finish line.

On Friday morning, Mr. Vaughan stopped by his office and shut the door. Bertram, looked up from the regional sales report he was consumed with in surprise, not used to impromptu visits from his boss.

"Can I speak with you?" Mr. Vaughan asked, formal as always, without a trace of indication as to whether the conversation would be positive or negative.

"Of course," Bertram replied, shoving the papers to the side as a way to clear his attention. Vaughan motioned to a chair with a raise of his eyebrows. "I'm sorry, yes, yes, please have a seat," Bertram fumbled, embarrassed that he hadn't offer a seat to his boss.

"Congratulations," Vaughan said simply, "nice work." Bertram looked at him blankly, confused. "You hit your quarterly number and then some," Vaughan said, producing a sheet of paper and handing it to Bertram.

"Wait, this is an order from NetCore... Is it, a mistake?" Bertram asked, confused.

Mr. Vaughan shook his head. "No, I just heard directly from Jerry Greenwell over there." Jerry was the Chief Operating Officer of NetCore and had been Dave's boss when he was still there. "Apparently, the company NetCore acquired can only handle about half of their orders adequately and still serve their other customers. Since you have maintained your relationship with them, Jerry wanted us to have the business."

Bertram was stunned. Marilyn Walker, a woman a little older than Bertram who had been promoted when Dave left, was someone that Bertram had stayed in contact with and periodically had helped answer a question if she needed something, even after NetCore had pulled its business. Even still, Bertram couldn't really see how they thought that was a big deal… he was just doing what was right. "Wow, I'm, surprised but very grateful. We might have just squeaked it out but now we definitely are on a good pace for the end of the year."

Mr. Vaughan nodded. "Agreed. Your pipeline has lots of good opportunity in it and I'm confident your team can hit this year's numbers." Vaughan paused and leaned back in his chair. "Bertram, there's actually something else I wanted to discuss with you." He reached into his jacket and pulled out an envelope, handing it to Bertram.

"Should I open it?" Bertram asked, taking the envelope somewhat tentatively.

Vaughan nodded. It was a check and a rather large one. Bertram looked at his boss, confused. He pursed his lips together. "I decided to give you a bonus to commemorate your progress. You worked very hard to achieve the thirty-five percent growth objective last year, even though it was a stretch. I was impressed with that. But I'm more impressed with your efforts through the first quarter. Even though this year's target is more aggressive, you've moved to make it happen and are positioned for success. This check is my way of telling you I've noticed."

Bertram was already calculating how much the bonus would accelerate his debt elimination, making it so that he'd be debt-free in two more months! Still stunned, Bertram stood to shake Mr. Vaughan's hand and thank him but Vaughan waved him back to his seat. Once Bertram was settled, Vaughan looked at him, considering him like an entomologist considering a somewhat rare grasshopper. He crossed his legs.

"Bertram, I have an opportunity that I'd like you to consider. Please keep this confidential as all of the pieces have not been decided and only a few of the individuals involved are aware." Vaughan looked at Bertram who registered his confirmation of the situation with a vigorous nod. Satisfied, Vaughan continued. "Sam Ferrante is retiring at the end of August and we'd like you to consider replacing him," he said without fanfare.

Ferrante was a larger-than-life person of unidentifiable age who always seemed to have a smile on his face. He had built the Southeast for the company and its revenues comprised more than one third of the overall revenue in the organization. Bertram could only manage a furrowed brow in immediate response, but knew how huge a promotion this was.

"If you are interested, you would be based in Tampa and would start there in July so that Sam could show you the ropes and introduce you to everyone. It's a big job but I think you're the right person for it," Vaughan handed Bertram a second envelope. "This details the pay and some of the other specifics of the position. You can read it and think about it for a couple of weeks. I will need an answer by April 15th." Vaughan tapped his palms on his knees to signal the meeting was over and moved to stand.

Bertram stood with him, still stunned by the entire meeting, and especially by the left-field promotion. "Thank you, Mr. Vaughan, I… I don't really know what to say," he managed.

Vaughan shrugged. "Yes would be fine," he offered with a wan smile.

"Thanks again," Bertram said, shaking his hand.

"Don't hesitate to reach out with questions in the meantime…" Vaughan said on his way out the door.

Bertram plopped back into his chair, overwhelmed by the emotions of the past week. Learning about Allen's illness, spending time with Bessie, getting an unexpected bonus that almost wiped out the rest of his debt, and a big new position was more than he could manage to process. He wasn't accustomed to being overwhelmed, but he felt that way at that moment and wasn't quite sure what to do with himself. As a distraction, he pulled out the check and his phone, using the new contribution to check his math and finding that if he used the whole amount of the check towards *'eliminating debt'*, he'd be debt-free by the end of May. He shook his head in disbelief, feeling a little lift in his spirits and a sense of pride.

"Wow," he said to himself, amazed at how quickly he'd gotten to a place where he could begin to move on to the final *'Money-Strong'* maxim: *'save the difference'*. Looking at the numbers in black and white, Bertram felt the same sense of accomplishment he used to get from the football field after a particularly well-executed game and it was both familiar and meaningful to get that kind of deep satisfaction. He noted that some of his previous exploits that seemed so exciting in the moment, including buying nice things or over-spending on an evening's festivities, didn't provide any lasting sense of achievement. Even the thrill of buying and driving around in his expensive BMW wore off within a few weeks. In a way, he was worried about opening the envelope outlining the offer of his new position, knowing that he'd have a hard time saying no to the money and prestige, while worrying that all of the people who seemed to really matter to him – Bessie, Allen, Norman to name a few – were very far away from Tampa, Florida.

Bertram hadn't yet talked to Allen about his illness, and he wasn't even sure how to bring it up. He spoke with both his mom and dad about it on Wednesday afternoon, looking for their input. His dad was limited in his advice but clearly felt like Bertram needed to wait until Allen was ready to talk to him about it, while his mom thought he should address it with him directly.

Bertram wasn't sure which way to go, knowing that Allen was a private person and that they were just now really getting to know each other. He decided to discuss it with him, hoping that Allen wouldn't find his inquiry an overreach but concerned that if it didn't get out in the open, he would have a limited ability to help or be involved in any way.

Bertram had kept the envelope containing his job offer sealed and sitting on his kitchen counter, not sure he was ready to introduce that option into his thinking. Every time he saw it propped up against the backsplash by the coffee maker he thought about how just a year ago, he probably would've jumped to accept the position before even reading the offer completely, his ego and pride thirsting for the recognition and the increased income. Now, with everything happening, this seemed like a better approach and he wanted to give himself some distance from his impulses before looking at it and considering the possibilities. Besides, all he wanted for the moment was to see if there was something he could do to help his brother and he didn't want a move to Tampa looming over there conversations. For now, he was content to wait.

Bertram pulled up to Allen and Gina's house and the girls were playing in the front yard. He couldn't quite tell what they were doing but whatever it was, they were squealing and running around, obviously enjoying each other's company. There was another girl with them, probably a neighbor's kid, that he didn't recognize but he waved at them all and took a deep breath to prepare himself for the conversation. The girls bounded over and gave him big hugs, introducing Amanda as their next-door neighbor's daughter who waved shyly, then they all turned around and began chasing each other again.

The springlike weather had reverted to the gray cold of a typical midwestern winter, but at least it wasn't raining or snowing and the promise of warmer weather had tipped its hat in acknowledgement.

Gina greeted Bertram at the door looking more tired than he had seen her, but he conceded that it could be his imagination based on the circumstances.

"Nice to see you, Bertram," she said, picking up a trail of items the girls had strewn about on the way towards the kitchen. "Allen is finishing his lunch if you want to say hi," she said, motioning him on while she headed towards a closet at the foot of the stairs with a mound of kid stuff. He helped her navigate opening the closet door and headed in to see his brother.

"Hey, Bertram," Allen said with surprise. "I didn't know you were stopping by today. Good to see you." Allen stood and pulled his brother in for his patented one-tap hug.

"Yeah, I was thinking I'd say 'hi' to mom and dad and thought I'd pop by here first," he fibbed, knowing full well that the entire purpose of his visit was to talk to Allen about his illness.

They made small talk for a bit, mostly consisting of Bertram updating his brother on a few superficial things, and then Allen suggested they go outside to survey the remaining portion of the fence that needed attention.

After walking around in the yard a while, Bertram decided to dive in. "So… I was talking to Mom about some stuff when I was here last," he started a little tenuously, "and, well, she shared what was going on."

Allen looked like some of the air went out of him. "What part?" he asked wearily.

"I mean… about your cancer," Bertram blurted. "She told me you have leukemia, but not a whole lot more." Bertram was happy to have the hard part out of the way.

Allen came back over to him and shoved his hands deep in his pockets, looking back at the house. "I would have preferred…" he trailed off and didn't finish the sentence, staying still. Bertram looked at his brother's lean profile, thinking he might have even lost a little more weight just over the last week since he'd seen him. "Yeah, I've got leukemia.

The girls don't know," Allen said, looking at his brother matter-of-factly.

After a pause, Bertram asked, "What's the prognosis…? Are you doing chemo or…"

Allen motioned him to the steps by the little tool shack and they sat down. "I just started chemo. I feel fine, maybe a little tired. It's not a big deal. I guess it's pretty advanced so they're recommending chemo and radiation," he shared.

Bertram looked at his brother. "What do you mean 'pretty advanced'?" he asked, swallowing hard. Allen shrugged and didn't answer.

Bertram sat with his brother, thinking about how unfair life could be and trying to be strong at the same time. He couldn't believe that this could happen just when he'd finally started to create a real relationship with Allen and that he was close enough to spend time with him.

He stayed quiet, even though he had a lot more questions. "I'd like to help in any way I can," Bertram said quietly. "Name it," he said, turning his head to look at his brother.

Allen smiled at him. "I appreciate that, Bertram. I'll try not to take you up on it." They both turned back to look at the house where the girls had just come out on the deck with a snack.

"Hi, Daddy! Hi, Uncle Bertram!" Layla, Allen's youngest waved energetically at them. Bertram and Allen waved back, smiling as well before looking briefly at each other.

At that moment, Bertram saw the pain in Allen's eyes and knew without a word that the leukemia was far more serious than his brother allowed. He nodded at Allen and they sat there watching the girls goof around, making it feel like for at least this moment, all was ok in the world.

On Monday morning while Bertram was sipping his first cup of coffee, he finally decided to look at the offer, still making its residence next to the coffee maker. In truth, he was a little surprised at himself. Given how success-minded he had always been, the fact that he almost didn't want to look at it seemed totally out of character, at least in the way he saw the world just a year ago. Bertram registered that things were so complicated at the moment, it wasn't completely bizarre that considering a big move and a larger job, although attractive, seemed at odds with other parts of his life.

He let out a big breath and opened the envelope. The terms of the offer were short and sweet, but they were also much more lucrative than he was expecting, so much so that his mouth got dry and he had to read the entire thing again slowly. The move to Tampa would mean a director's title, a fifty percent increase in salary and the opportunity to earn over one hundred percent more in bonuses. Not only that, the company would pay all of his moving expenses and provide an auto allowance, something he hadn't received at all in the past. It was a whopper of an offer.

Bertram loved the changing seasons when he was a kid and always had thought that were he to have kids of his own, it would be fun to raise them in a place where they could make snow angels and watch the leaves turn. As he got older though, the idea of living in a warmer climate had become much more appealing and he had even mulled it over well before the Tampa offer came up.

Prior to his friendship with Norman took shape and his first chance meeting with Bessie, he had gotten a job offer from a young company in Orlando that was looking for people with his background and resume. One of the assistant coaches from his college-football days who had stayed in touch with him had also stayed in touch with another former athlete who was one of the founders. Bertram seriously considered the position and got to know central Florida a little while he was interviewing, ultimately deciding that his current job provided more immediate opportunity and declining the offer. Although he wasn't interested in that particular job, walking around in short sleeves in February when nothing short of a parka would do at home was eye-opening and lodged in his mind as something that might seem more attractive than he had given it credit for. As a result, the Tampa location, apart from being far from all of the people he loved, was also a selling point.

Wishing he'd never opened the envelope, Bertram headed off to the office, chatting briefly with Norman on the way out. He was running behind for the weekly pipeline meeting so they didn't have a chance to catch up meaningfully and Bertram suggested they find time to talk later in the week. He had a lot to get his friend caught up on and could use his practical advice in a number of areas of his life. They scheduled time early on Thursday morning to share their morning cup of coffee together since Archie could cover for a bit and Bertram rushed off to the office to avoid being later for his own meeting.

Late in the day on Wednesday, just as Bertram was wrapping up for the evening, Mr. Vaughan stopped by on his way out the door. He knocked lightly on the open door before entering.

"Got a minute?" Mr. Vaughan asked pleasantly.

"Sure, I was just trying to tidy up things around here a little," Bertram said, looking at the mess of little stacks of papers occupying various corners of his work area. "End of the quarter seems to have gotten the best of me," he said in resignation to the entropy surrounding him.

Vaughan gave a compassionate little chuckle despite the fact that there was never a single piece of wayward paper visible anywhere in his office at the end of any day. "Did you have a chance to review the offer and did you have any questions? You've still got a couple of weeks for a final decision, but I thought I'd check and see if you needed something clarified."

"Thanks Mr. Vaughan. No, it seemed very simple and clear and quite generous if I'm honest. I don't have any questions." Bertram's heart was pounding and he wanted to be extremely careful about what he said since he had literally no clue what to do at that point.

Vaughan gave a little wave of understanding. "No problem, take your time. It's a big decision and comes with a lot of responsibility. Not that what you're doing now is easy, far from it, but the Southeast adds a whole layer of expectation and stress. You can do it and do it very well. You just have to be sure you want it. Anyway, I've got to run, see you in the morning," he said, walking out as Bertram said goodnight.

Bertram was never more torn about any decision in his life. The Tampa job was a rarified, maybe even once-in-a-lifetime position, something that could send his career on an entirely new path at a whole other level. From the perspective of a young, ambitious, go-getter, it was a total no-brainer. If he stayed true to the '*Money-Strong*' methods, he could save quite a bit more money and quickly add to his financial fitness level, even while living a very nice lifestyle and enjoying better weather. It seemed hard to argue with the financial value of the move on any level. On the other hand, he still hadn't completed all the '*Money-Strong*' maxims, so he had some concern that he'd use the heady new job and income to get himself into even bigger problems down the road and knew that it would take real vigilance to avoid making easy, but poor, financial decisions.

More importantly, his relationships were starting to matter a lot to him, more than they ever had in his life. Norman was becoming both a true friend and a mentor and Bertram felt very close to him, knowing that he was a better person for their relationship. His love for Bessie was real and he wasn't ready to give up on their relationship, even with the reality of her marriage looming in the near future.

If all that weren't enough, he wanted to be as involved and available as he could to Allen and his family, especially through the next few months as he pursued his treatments, not sure how he could help but being committed to whatever his brother needed. The distraction of a pending move, a new job, and the thousand or so miles between them if he ended up in Tampa, would make it almost impossible to provide any real value during the critical months of Allen's fight with the disease. Even being optimistic, Bertram knew it would diminish his ability to be present in a meaningful way. Plus, given how stoic his brother could be, he guessed that he would have to take things on without being asked, rather than waiting for Allen to wave the flag; not something easily done from afar.

Early Thursday morning, Bertram had just filled a mug with coffee when Norman knocked softly at the door, trying not to disturb the neighbors who may be luckily sleeping in a bit. Bertram let him in and gave him a big hug, knowing better than to ask if Norman needed coffee since he always brought his from home. They chatted easily for a few minutes and Bertram did his best to get Norman caught up about Allen's condition and his time with Bessie. Norman was somber and concerned, mostly listening. Then, Bertram spun around to the conversation about the new job offer, sharing the details and some of his concerns. Again, Norman listened quietly, asking a question or two, but not offering up much.

"I guess I'm really in a difficult spot and not really sure

what to do. The timing is horrible, but I also feel that the opportunity is almost too good to pass up," Bertram said, with more of a question than a statement.

Norman sat up from where he was resting with his back against the couch cushions and took a sip of coffee, placing the mug back on the coffee table and leaning back again. "Bertram, remind me, when do you *eliminate debt* completely?"

Bertram looked confused. "Next month... With the bonus I was able to speed things up and I'm just going to add some money and get rid of it," he said.

Norman nodded appreciatively. "Good, that's real good, Bertram. You've done a great job there—"

Bertram interrupted, "—yes and I can't believe how much money I could save if I took the new job. Not only could I *'save the difference'* of what I used to pay to support my monthly debt payments, but I also could *'save the difference'* in added income. Pretty soon I'd have a lot of money."

"That's true, you could save a lot more. But over time you'd earn more money here as well and with the gradual increase in your income, you'll be a lot less likely to overspend," Norman pointed out.

"Yes, I've thought of that as well," Bertram conceded. "I'm not sure I fully trust myself to do the right thing once I make a lot more money overnight."

Norman nodded. "Yes, there's a reason that winning the lottery actually increases your chances of going bankrupt... It's because getting a lot of money at once without learning how to manage it is very dangerous for most people. You've definitely learned some good skills, but it's very easy to slide back into bad habits. And don't forget, *'saving the difference'* isn't always as easy for people as it sounds. I've seen people pay off debt but still spend almost all of their extra money instead of saving it."

Bertram nodded, almost to himself, seeing how that could happen. "I guess it is pretty tempting when you have that extra money and you're not being forced into paying debt off. How do you make sure it goes where it's supposed to?"

"Good question. What you do is, you set up an automatic payment in the exact amount you are going to save every month from your checking account to your investment account. You set the payments to coincide with your payroll so the money doesn't gather dust in your checking account. Depending on how you're paid, you might need two automatic payments, but basically it's that simple. A recurring payment, at the same time every month, in the exact amount you want to save, from checking to your investment account. In your case, since you're paid twice monthly, you'd set up two of these payments to coincide with your pay dates."

"If I took the Tampa job, couldn't I just apply that same approach to the excess salary? Wouldn't I just add the additional amount to my automatic transfer and send it all to my investment account?" Bertram asked, testing his friend's logic.

"Yes, that's exactly right. Using that method would make it much more likely that you wouldn't squander your additional earnings and would save the extra money," Norman agreed.

Bertram considered that a moment. "Man, I'd save like crazy if I did that," he thought out loud, shaking his head in astonishment.

"That's true," Norman responded. "So long as you set it up automatically and didn't count on yourself to make good choices, you could save a ton of money that way."

"There's something else worth considering," Norman continued after a moment. "Once you set yourself up on 'saving the difference', you can always continue to add money to the automatic savings plan. Every time you get a raise, you can increase what you contribute. And because the amount ends up being fairly significant to start with, since you have no debts to pay and have rolled up all of those payments, you still will end up with a ton of money over time. Having money gives you the ability to make choices that aren't about money at all… like where you live or who you spend your time with. No question, you can make more money if you move to Tampa for this new position, but if you stay you will still end up being very financially secure over time." Norman looked at Bertram to see if what he was saying was sinking in.

"You mean, because I'm saving aggressively, whether I'm here or in Tampa, I'm still going to have financial freedom eventually?" Bertram asked.

"Yes, but also that having the ability to save diligently once you '*eliminate debt*' gives you the ability to make choices for other reasons. You'll make more money in Tampa, no question. And you may save more as well. But will you have more of a life? Will you be surrounded by the things and people that actually matter to you?" Norman paused to allow his question to have its impact.

"Bertram, being '*Money-Strong*' is actually about love. '*Eliminating debt*' and '*saving the difference*' give you the power to make the choices you care about; to be with the people you care about. You don't just have to climb to the next rung on any ladder… you can look and see where the ladder is leading and climb a different one entirely. I'm not saying you should stay or go – that is your decision entirely, even though I would miss you quite a bit. What I am saying is that the entire point of becoming '*Money-Strong*' is to have the ability to live how, where, and with whom you want. That's the real point of this whole thing," Norman stated, speaking more emotionally than usual. He looked at his watch. "Are you going to be late for work?"

"No, I'm ok, thanks, Norman," Bertram said somewhat absentmindedly, all of the choices and conversation whirling around in his head like a smoothie in a food processor.

"I should probably relieve Archie or he'll be cross with me all day," Norman joked, knowing that Archie never loved the mornings, since he was much more comfortable fixing inanimate objects than interacting with other members of the same species.

They walked to the door and Norman turned to face his friend. "I'll love you no matter what you choose, Bertram. Just be sure you make the decision for the right reasons and it will always be a good one," he said, laying one of his mammoth hands on Bertram's shoulder. They gave each other a hug and said goodbye.

The next couple of weeks were challenging. Bertram felt the pressure of the looming decision regarding his promotion, even though he was too busy to give it much detailed consideration. Sam Ferrante had called Bertram out of the blue one day during the first week of April, hoping he could help to describe the opportunity and provide some insight into the area. Sam had raised his family in Tampa and was a transplant from New York, where his large extended family all lived within a twenty-block radius, so he knew the difficulty of leaving a community with deep roots. It was a pleasant conversation and it was also quite clear that Sam really wanted Bertram to seriously consider the opportunity, hesitant to leave the twenty years of work he'd put into building the Southeast to someone less capable. Although Sam didn't come out and directly say it, there was little doubt from the nature of the call that Sam had been influential in suggesting Bertram for the job and was fairly married to the idea of him taking it.

Allen's latest test results were coming back in a few days and Bertram thought the cumulative effects of the chemo on his body were becoming more obvious, which would shortly make it harder for him to hide his illness from the girls. With Bertram's encouragement, Gina and Allen had elected to tell them that Allen was ill, while coming up with a plan to downplay the seriousness of the situation. Despite this, the kids managed to sniff it out and seemed to take it hard even though they didn't fully understand it.

For all of Allen's obvious strengths, including the ability to fix nearly anything, a deep knowledge of all things mechanical and a deceiving amount of physical ability given his slender frame, the most overlooked one may have been his ability to be fully present for his kids. He was perfectly content doing whatever it was they wanted to do and could often be found with stuffed animals stacked on top of him or reading a book to them for the fiftieth time. The illness had already taken some of that away, making him incredibly exhausted and physically ill. As was his nature, he would push through those moments as much as he could, but it was clear that something was different.

The same day that Bertram had the chat with Sam, he got a save-the-date notice from Bessie with her wedding announcement. Seeing the pictures of Bessie and Tom standing in front of a peony garden, in a gazebo, and doing other normal couple things made something deep within him crumble off, like old mortar falling from a wall without provocation. He knew that she was engaged and had heard from his mother that they were thinking about getting married next spring, but he wasn't fully prepared for his reaction to seeing it all with such formality.

All of these things colored the sense of pride Bertram experienced when he made his last debt payment. He had expected that moment to be a little celebration of sorts, but it wasn't much more than the click of a mouse and a small distraction. He was thankful to have completed the milestone, yet the lack of fanfare he felt seemed a little anticlimactic and disappointing. With his mind on so many other things, he forgot to set up the automatic monthly transfer out of his checking account that Norman had discussed with him to begin his work on the fifth milestone: '*save the difference*'. When it did cross his mind a little later in the week, Bertram also found himself a little confused about what exactly to do with the money he was saving. Would he invest it? If so, where and how? He figured he would see Norman sometime soon and get some guidance on all that.

A week before Bertram owed a final decision to Mr. Vaughan around his promotion, Bertram went to Weaver to visit Allen. It had been about two weeks since he had seen him last but it was clear that he continued to lose his stamina and he was still shedding weight, largely because he had no appetite.

Although Bertram had been worried from the moment he had heard about Allen's illness, this visit cemented that concern in a very real way. They spent some time watching the kids play various games in the backyard while sipping on an iced tea but Allen didn't participate in the activities like he would have in the past, not having the energy to leave the deck. At one point, Allen looked at Bertram for a long minute.

"What?" Bertram asked, a little unnerved by his brother's attention.

Allen didn't break his gaze. "You've grown into a fine young man," he said, sounding at least ten years older than he was, but sincere at the same time.

"Thank you," Bertram said, trying not to show how much his brother's approval meant to him.

"Bertram, I'm dying."

"What are you talking about, you're going to beat this thing!" Bertram retorted, mad that his brother would even think those kind of thoughts at that point.

"Bertram, this is far along. We caught it late. I know I won't make it more than a few months but I'm going to go through the motions regardless. I have a lot to live for." Allen's gaze wandered out to his children, laughing hysterically at some mishap during their spontaneously invented game, and then to the house and the sky as well. "But I'm not afraid of dying. I only want my family to be taken care of... and my modest savings and life insurance should take care of most of that. I hope that Gina can find someone else at some point and that the girls..." Allen's voice tapered off.

Bertram was trying very hard to hold himself together, especially since the girls would be alarmed if tough Uncle Bertram started crying. He looked away and blinked his grief back into his body. "How can I help?" he finally asked.

Allen looked at his brother with a tired smile. "You already are," he said, turning back to watch the kids for a minute. "When I'm gone, Gina is going to need a bunch of help getting things in order. Mom and Dad will help but maybe you can too... It's the only thing I'm really worried about – how she and the kids will be in those first few months, especially." He shrugged. "Other than that, I think it's all pretty straightforward."

Bertram nodded. "I really hope you fight like heck, Allen. You can beat this thing if you..."

Allen held up his hand. "Bertram, there's no doubt I will fight, and maybe that will buy me some extra time. But I can feel my body failing and I don't want to delude myself or anyone else. However many days I have left, I'll use them as best I can. That's the most I'm able to promise."

Bertram reached over and gripped his brother's forearm, surprised at how thin it felt in his hand. They sat there like

---

that, enjoying each other's company, letting the April sun warm them, both lost in their own version of what was happening in their lives.

Bertram stayed for dinner and after everything was cleaned up and put away, Allen poured them each a couple of fingers of bourbon and motioned him out to the family room. Bertram looked at his brother with a grimace. "I have zero doubt that bourbon is not on your 'approved foods' list," he said, putting his hands on his hips for effect. Allen snickered, and shoved the glass at him. Bertram shook his head but eventually took it and they went out to sit for a moment before Bertram headed back out to the city.

"Thanks for coming over, Bertram, it really is great to spend some time together. Wish I was feeling better so I could've put you to work today," Allen joked.

Bertram laughed. "Just let me know what you need next time – you can bark orders at me from a deck chair." They both chuckled.

"What's new at work?" Allen asked, changing direction.

Bertram wasn't sure how to answer… He didn't really want to share the Tampa opportunity for fear that Allen would feel responsible for him not taking it. "It's been… fine. Good really. I got an unexpected bonus which allowed me to pay off all of the rest of my debt, so now I'm starting to save some money for the first time in my life." He thought talking about 'Money-Strong' would be a safe and reasonable way to answer Allen's question without wading into the conversation about Tampa.

Allen seemed pleased that Bertram had put so much energy into fixing his financial situation. Although he had never been specific with Bertram about it in the past, Allen shared that he and Gina never had made much money, but had always lived frugally and had invested wisely for the future. Recent circumstances made these decisions more poignant, Bertram reflected, since instead of having a nice retirement together, it seemed likely to Allen that the money would be a part of insuring the future for Gina and the kids once he was gone. They spent some time chatting about the other elements of the '*Money-Strong Creed*' and Norman and Irma while they sipped the last of their bourbons.

"Saving money is not something I would have expected us to share," Allen said without judgement. "Seemed to me that you were interested in a much higher-flying life than that… It's a good change and a smart decision. What caused you to get serious about it?" Allen tried to milk a last drop out of his glass. "No way I'll get Gina to let me have another," he explained to his brother conspiratorially."

Bertram summed up the experience of bumping into Bessie and recognizing his feelings for her and the timing of his conversations with Norman. "I guess it just seemed that more than one thing in my life was pointing towards me getting my money issues resolved and it was getting hard to ignore," he said.

Allen shifted in his chair. "I'm happy for you, Bertram, and your life will be way more fulfilling now that you've given yourself choices. I've seen too many people make bad financial decisions that forced them to stay in a job they couldn't stand or in a bad relationship because there wasn't an alternative," he said approvingly.

"Thanks, Allen, that means a lot to me. I guess… there's one other thing… I could use your opinion I think." He swirled his empty glass around, still not sure sharing the Tampa development would be a great idea, but really valuing his brother's opinion.

Allen didn't reply, waiting for his brother to spit it out. Bertram ran through the whole thing fairly quickly, giving Allen the top-level information and the numbers. Allen didn't react at all, other than a short low-pitched virtually inaudible whistle when Bertram dropped the numbers on him.

"Yeah," Bertram acknowledged, "it's a ton of money."

Allen nodded. "More than I've ever made and I'm ten years older than you!" he pointed out, with pride instead of envy.

"Pretty unbelievable," Bertram agreed. "The thing is… I've got a lot here that matters to me. You, the girls, Bessie and Norman… not to mention Mom and Dad who aren't getting any younger. It's really not as easy a decision as it would have been even a year ago when I probably already would be on a plane to Tampa," Bertram said honestly.

Allen considered that briefly. "I'm sure this will sound bad, but you know I'm not much for ceremony. Bertram, I'm not going to be around that much longer… and it looks like Bessie is getting married… If you are attracted to this job, you should take it," Allen declared simply.

"Well, it's not… I guess maybe it's not quite that simple to me. There's still your treatment and Gina and the girls. Not to mention Norman and Mom and Dad…" Bertram replied.

"All I know, Bertram, is, I took a safe and simple road in my life and I have no regrets. In fact I've been largely very happy and content. You've always been more ambitious… and probably had more talent. You should do what's right for you… and not what I or anyone else think you should do. So long as you keep living within the, what's Norman's money thing called?" Allen said searching for the words.

"You mean the '*Money-Strong Creed*'?" Bertram offered.

"Yes. Being financially secure makes the difference no matter what your choices… Who knows? Maybe you'll even go into business for yourself one day. But you can follow the *Creed* anywhere. In terms of this opportunity, the only question is whether you want the job and whether you want to live in Tampa in my mind. You can work around the other stuff," Allen said, obviously getting tired.

Bertram looked at the time and got ready to leave, figuring

they had to start working on getting the kids to bed anyway. After saying goodbye to Gina and the girls, Allen walked him to the door, shuffling a little more than Bertram remembered. They gave each other a more heartfelt hug than usual, foregoing the one-tap bro version Allen seemed to prefer.

"Bertram, I appreciate you. And I love you. If you love that girl, I think you've got to tell her what's on your mind and in your heart and see what happens. If it's not meant to be, then maybe you should take the job."

Bertram didn't reply and looked out at the night from the front porch. "Thanks, Allen. I love you too." He turned and walked towards his car so his brother wouldn't have to share the depth of his pain.

Bertram was shaken a little by his visit with Allen. Although he was just getting to know him deeply, Allen's comfortable resignation to the disease that was ravaging his body made it hard to stay positive about his prospects of returning to health.

Bertram's college head coach always used to say, "I can't want this more than you do," when he was frustrated with a player's performance either on or off the field. This saying swam around Bertram's head in relation to the situation with Allen, as he was willing his brother to fight, while his brother seemed to be comfortable being passive. He wasn't going to give up on influencing him to change his mindset, figuring anything positive would probably help his chances.

With his Tampa decision sneaking up on him, he knew he had to have a serious conversation with Bessie. While he'd told her his feelings for her in a general way, he'd never laid it all out on the table and he had made the commitment to himself to do just that. He figured it was like the long bomb end around that helped his Weaver High varsity football team make the playoffs when he was a freshman – it probably wouldn't work but if it did it would change everything. The odds were about the same but since the football game ended in one of the most unlikely upsets in the school's history, he figured the conversation had at least that much of a chance for success.

After a few text trails, Bertram set up a time to visit with Bessie that would allow him to pop by and check in on Allen as well. He wasn't exactly sure what the right venue would be for the conversation and was worried that he'd scare Bessie off if it seemed anything remotely like a date. They decided to grab a couple of burritos at a newer Mexican restaurant in town just off of the plaza which had outside seating. It was over-lorded by a few big heat lamps that made the still chilly evening weather tolerable. Bertram was running a few minutes behind and texted Bessie his order, pulling into the restaurant just as the food was coming out.

"Hi, Bessie," Bertram said out of breath, bustling into the restaurant to help her carry their order. "Sorry I'm late, I went with Allen to pick up the kids at soccer practice which was probably a mistake," he explained, grabbing some extra napkins.

"No biggie, I was barely ahead of you… We're trying to wrap up assessments before Easter break and it's been nutso at school too," Bessie conceded.

They found an empty table positioned right under one of the heaters and away from the other guests scattered about the patio and got settled.

"Man, these chips are so good," Bessie said with some reverence. "They fry them fresh every day and I'm sort of addicted to them."

Bertram laughed but couldn't answer because he'd just shoveled a few of them in his mouth, causing Bessie to giggle as well. They ate quietly for a few more moments, feeling the comfort of having known each other as long as they were conscious.

Bessie told Bertram about the school year and some of the preliminary wedding plans while Bertram shared the happenings in his life and Allen's status, leaving out the part about Tampa and the primary purpose for his visit.

After they had properly caught up, Bertram took a deep breath and plunged in.

"Bessie, I have to talk to you about something that's been on my mind, even though I'm not super-comfortable about it," he started honestly. Bessie looked at him, setting down the last bite or two of her burrito. "First, I want to say that I know you may not feel quite the same way about me that I feel about you and that's fine. But I know you have feelings for me, and I think they're not too much different than my own or I wouldn't even talk to you about this." He looked at her for a reaction but couldn't really read one so he kept on.

"Anyway, I realize that you think we're different people in terms of lifestyles and maybe even values… and I admit, that may have been true for quite a while. But it isn't true anymore. I've fully committed to the '*Money-Strong Creed*' Norman has helped me with and I even just got completely out of debt. To be clear, although I may have started down that path to impress you, I've continued down the path completely for myself. I want to be free from financial stress and have the choices that money strength will allow. Watching what has been going on with Allen and his family only makes me even more committed to a life of lowered expectations and financial security," he said resolutely.

Bessie looked at him encouragingly but said nothing, wrapping her jacket around her as the temperature dropped.

"Are you warm enough?" Bertram paused to check on her, wriggling free of his own jacket to help.

"No, no, I'm fine," Bessie said, waving him back to his seat. "Really, please, I'm good," she reiterated. Bertram sat down but left the jacket draped on her lap and she didn't move to give it back.

"Anyway," he said, resettling, "I just wanted you to know how serious I am about creating a financially fit life, especially because I know how important that is to you and you haven't always seen me that way."

A bus boy came by and asked if they were through and they both said they weren't quite sure, thanking him.

"I'm really glad you've found Norman and turned your financial life around. In fact, I think it's pretty brave," Bessie said. "Trading in that fancy car and moving to a smaller apartment must've been hard for you."

"Actually, thinking about doing all those things was really hard but once I had moved, traded in the car, and changed my lifestyle, I found it surprisingly liberating," Bertram said, shrugging a little. "I don't miss any of it. And paying off my debt while beginning to save money for the first time makes me really proud," he added. Bessie nodded in understanding. "There is one other main thing I need to say though. I should've said it before but instead I danced around it, and I need to say it now." Bertram began to get to the punch line, ready to fade back and fling the football all those yards towards the end zone.

"Bertram," Bessie tried to interject, sensing the direction of the conversation.

"Please, Bessie, let me get this out. I really need to tell you this and I won't have another chance." She let herself lean back to her seat, still visibly agitated. "The thing is, I'm totally and completely in love with you. It's not the kind of love that goes away because it's like the rings of a big redwood tree, each circle representing every year and getting wider all the time. I don't know if you're in love with me, but I think you are. I'm also sure this conversation makes your life more complicated no matter how you respond and for that I'm really sorry. But I also know that I *am* the man you want me to be, even if you're not so convinced, and I want to spend my life with you. Could you get past my history and take a chance? Would you want to?" Bertram was looking at Bessie with all of the attention in the world and her eyes were rimmed with tears.

Bessie couldn't respond for a number of minutes, feeling emotional and slightly embarrassed about it. "Bertram, I do love you," she admitted. "And it's clear that you've come a long way. I really appreciate that and am proud of you." She hesitated a little. "But Bertram, I'm engaged to someone I truly care about, someone who is steady and safe and I know shares many of the same interests and aspirations I have. You... well, honestly, you scare me a little and I worry that we aren't really suited for each other for the long-term. I want a simple life and I think you still want more." Bessie grabbed Bertram's hand. "I guess, it's... that I just don't know if I have the courage for us to be together. I'm sorry." Bessie pulled away her hand and they both sat there processing the conversation, each lost in their own thoughts.

Finally, Bertram broke the silence. "Bessie, are you in love with me?" he asked bluntly.

She nodded but couldn't speak.

"Then how can we not be together? You'd rather be safe than happy?"

Bessie looked out towards the plaza where the sidewalk lights and a light wind made the willow branches of the plazas many trees look as if they were waltzing to a minuet crafted solely for them and then slowly back at Bertram. "I don't know, Bertram. It's just... it's not simple like that for me," she said.

He nodded and decided not to push her further, content that they spend a few more moments together before the both of them would have to get back to their lives, watching the trees turn the plaza into a ballroom.

Bertram got to the office early on the day he was supposed to inform the company of his intentions. He had tossed and turned most of the night, still unsure as to what he wanted to do. If the conversation with Bessie had gone differently, it would have been a much easier choice to stay in his current role but without firm resolution there, his path was less clear. What made the situation even more complicated was the fact that Bessie hadn't given him a clear 'no'. It seemed quite obvious to Bertram that she was in love with him but that her anxiety around his past decisions, her own family trauma, coupled with her impending marriage to someone safe, all conspired against her following her heart. Bertram's biggest fear was that Bessie might come around to the idea of taking a leap with him and that he would already be in Tampa, making it impossible. Then there was the situation with Allen whom he didn't want to abandon, especially at this stage of his treatment. With everything up in the air, making a huge life-changing decision was that much more difficult.

Mr. Vaughan had put Bertram on his schedule for ten-thirty, and up until about ten-fifteen, Bertram still hadn't decisively made up his mind. He paced in his office a little, unable to settle down, hoping some movement would calm his nerves. At the appointed time, he wandered into Mr. Vaughan's office and sat down, waiting for his boss to complete the email he was writing. Vaughan held up an index finger to indicate that he was just about finished, the room quiet with the exception of the clicking of his keyboard. "Thanks for waiting, Bertram," Vaughan said, turning to face him and shake his hand. "So, what did you decide on the big Tampa move?"

Though Mr. Vaughan was never one for preliminaries, the speed with which he cut to the chase still took Bertram a little by surprise. "Well, I'd love to tell you I've come to an answer... and in a way I guess I have. But I'd like to talk to you openly about what's going on in my life so the answer will make sense. Is that ok?" Bertram asked.

Vaughan cocked his head to the side and furrowed his brow a bit, like he was studying the peculiar behavior of a colorful bird in the wild. He opened his hand in an invitation to continue.

"Not sure where to begin, so I'll just cut to the important parts. I really want the job. It's a great opportunity, the pay package is extremely fair, and I've toyed with a move to a warmer climate. It should be a no-brainer. But unfortunately... it isn't quite so easy. I'm quite serious about a girl who has deep roots here and she... she isn't so sure about me yet. A move would basically pull me out of the game in the fourth quarter. Also, my older brother is very sick. He has leukemia and it is pretty advanced. I'm not sure what's going to happen there, but I can't bring myself to leave right now. Obviously, things could change in his condition, for the better or worse, before I would need to be present in Florida and that might mean that I could take on the role at the proposed start time. But since I can't count on that happening, I'm stuck with a very tough decision." Bertram paused to reel in his emotions while Mr. Vaughan sat quietly with his hands forming a teepee in front of his chest and his elbows resting on his chair arms.

"If the job started next year, or it were closer to home or the things in my life weren't so crazy, I would be thrilled to accept it. Unfortunately, under the circumstances, I'm going to have to decline it."

Bertram could barely listen to his refusal and hoped he wasn't making one of the dumbest decisions of his life. He'd made the mistake of using one of those online calculators to analyze how much more money he could save with the new position's increased salary and it was shocking, especially after using the little compounding tool to see what happened to the money as it grew over the years.

Mr. Vaughan took a couple of moments to respond, clearly surprised about Bertram's decision. "I appreciate you sharing all of that with me, and I'm very sorry to hear about your brother. I lost my father last year and it was very difficult so I know a little about what you're going through. In terms of Tampa, I wish we could wait until the first of the year, but Sam's retirement date coincides with an extended trip he will take for his honeymoon and we will need someone in the role in time to get familiar with the job before he's gone," Vaughan said.

Bertram nodded understandingly. He knew that Sam was planning to marry his longtime girlfriend, having put it off for years because the sting of a nasty divorce had long lingered.

Vaughan looked at Bertram, considering him. "Are you totally sure this is what you want to do?" he asked.

"Yes, given the circumstances it is. If the job were local or the things in my life were different right now, it would be a totally different story. I can't tell you how hard this job is to turn down..." Bertram looked like he could hardly believe what he was doing, like some puppet master had taken him over and he was just responding to the tugging of the strings.

"Well, I'll let the executive team and Sam know later today. They'll be disappointed... The second-in-line candidate was a distant second," Vaughan shared, stating a fact without a hint of intended flattery.

"That's comforting to know," Bertram replied, laughing. "In all seriousness, I hope I get another opportunity at some point in the future, and hope I continue to earn your trust and respect. Turning down something like this feels a little like career suicide."

"Don't worry, just keep doing what you're doing. Things will come up… and you will still be in line for something when they do," Vaughan said, waving off Bertram's concern. "You're off to a strong start this year and I'm sure you'll finish strong based on the pipeline and your efforts." Vaughan stood and shook Bertram's hand. "Please let me know how your brother is doing when you know more. I admire that you are willing to sacrifice your immediate term upside for your family and I recognize how tough this decision was for you. I'm not sure how I would have operated in the same situation," Vaughan said in a rare moment of personal connection, surprising Bertram with the sincerity of it.

"Thanks Mr. Vaughan, that means a lot to me," Bertram replied, shaking his hand again before walking towards the door.

"Oh, and Bertram." Bertram turned back. "I hope you get the girl," Vaughan said, with the barest threat of something close to a smile.

Bertram wasn't really sure how to set up his investment plan so he could '*save the difference*' that he used to spend on his monthly payments. Since Norman had said to make it automatic, he just thought he'd set up the automatic transfer to pull the money from his checking account into his savings. While he was inputting the entry into his banking software, he couldn't help having a pang of regret since the number would have been so much larger had he accepted the Tampa job. Bertram didn't allow himself to linger on that feeling for long and moved on, finishing the task and closing the app.

He figured there was a better way to invest the money since his savings account earned barely any interest, but he had no idea what that was. Norman had mentioned previously that he could help him understand how to invest and Bertram wanted to share an update on the current status of the other things in his life anyway. Bertram gave him a quick call and Norman suggested that he come pick Bertram up on Saturday morning so that they could catch up and then head over to meet someone that he wanted to participate in the conversation. Bertram resisted the urge to ask more questions and they settled on nine o'clock.

Bertram was waiting outside when Norman pulled up, hopping into the passenger seat quickly so he didn't have to park. The spring air was warm enough that he had been comfortable sitting outside with a light jacket and he enjoyed a few quiet minutes of sunbathing while awaiting Norman's arrival.

"Hi, Bertram." Norman reached over and squeezed his shoulder in greeting while pulling back out into traffic.

"Hey, Norman." Bertram patted his friend's hand in response.

"Where are we headed?"

Norman smiled impishly. "You'll find out in a minute, mister ants-in-your-pants," he teased. "In the meantime, get me up to speed."

Bertram filled Norman in on all of the latest events including his decision to pass on the Tampa opportunity. Norman listened patiently, nodding at the right times.

"I guess that's about it," Bertram said, wrapping up his

update. "Still no real idea what's going to happen with Bessie, but it doesn't look great. Not giving up yet," he added, as if verbalizing it might will his preferred outcome into existence.

"Man, that's a lot to be sorting through," Norman marveled. "How did it feel to pass on Tampa?"

Bertram ran his hand through what there was of his tightly trimmed hair. "Like I was doing something for the right reasons that felt all wrong," he said, hoping Norman understood. Norman didn't respond, in a signal of both recognition and empathy.

Bertram had been talking so much, he hadn't fully been paying attention to where they were. They had been going south on the interstate for a time and had pulled off into a wooded area with rolling hills. From the look of things, they were in Dunhaven, an enclave of gated estate homes with large plots of land that tended to be occupied by families with long histories in the area. "Did you buy me a present?" Bertram joked, gawking at a particularly stunning home with an equestrian facility as they passed it. Norman chuckled.

A few minutes later they turned into a driveway that was almost hidden and stopped at a wrought-iron gate with what looked like a large ancient gas lantern hanging high above it. Behind the gate, far down the swerving brick road trimmed with towering trees before giving way to an expanse of lawn, stood an incredible Georgian-style mansion, looking like it had been there since Lincoln was in office.

"We're going here?" Bertram said in amazement, Norman just looking over at him as the automatic gate swung open magically, lightly touching the gas as they cruised up the drive into the carriage circle in front of the house and parked. An enormous portico stretched out over the driveway held up by columns whose feet were embedded in a small island overflowing with flowers and centered by a stone fountain. Under the overhang dripped the largest chandelier Bertram had ever seen; so massive he stood beneath it in awe as he got out of the car. Norman watched his friend's reaction with a smile, finally leading him to the front door which opened before they rang.

"Norman!" the beautifully elegant woman who opened it exclaimed, immediately wrapping her arms around him, almost disappearing in his embrace. She then turned her sharply flinted blue eyes to Bertram, smiling widely. "And you must be Bertram," she said, extending a hand and shaking his firmly enough to convey confidence while lacking real formality. "It's so nice to finally meet you. I'm Naomi."

Something about this woman was unlike any person Bertram had ever experienced and he could barely respond with more than a thank you. The whole experience so far was a little overwhelming and he touched his clothing, suddenly feeling vastly underdressed, even though Naomi was wearing nothing more elaborate than jeans and a light sweater.

"Please, you two, come on in." She motioned them over to a sitting area that looked out on a resort-style pool, past which was an incredible garden with a very slight slope, eventually leading down to a thick wooded area somewhere the length of a football field in the distance. "Care for tea or coffee? Water?" Naomi motioned to a well-stocked coffee table and they all found seats and got settled.

Naomi and Norman made some small talk, catching up briefly on people they had in common as Bertram tried to piece together who this woman was, how Norman might know her, and what on earth they were doing in her living quarters.

After a few moments, Norman described why he had brought Bertram over. "Naomi, Bertram here has just graduated to stage five of the *'Money-Strong Creed'*," Norman began.

"Oh, that's wonderful, so he's already *'saving the difference',*" Naomi interrupted enthusiastically.

"Yes, that's right. He's on the path, for sure. I thought he might be sick of me explaining things and that you would be a much better person to talk to him about how to invest that money – especially given how good you are at it," Norman explained.

Naomi laughed. "That's great, I'm happy to help." she shifted her powerful gaze to Bertram and sat forward on the chair.

A boy of about ten came in from somewhere behind Bertram and gave her, and then Norman, a big hug – letting her know that he was going with his dad to his soccer game. He introduced himself politely to Bertram and disappeared.

"Wow, he's gotten big," Norman said shaking his head. "I've got to come around more often!"

Naomi smiled somewhat wistfully and just nodded, looking mortal for a nanosecond, then turned back to Bertram. "I first probably should explain something that might help to give a little context," she suggested. "I was married very young and had a baby, who is now almost thirty, dropping out of college so that I could help to support us. My husband was a good man, but we were both young and couldn't work through the stresses of being poor parents who were still children themselves. After a few years together we split up and I was left with the prospect of raising a child as a single mom."

Naomi poured a half a cup of coffee, stirred in a touch of sugar and sat back into the plush couch while Bertram was unsuccessfully attempting to get his head around Naomi being poor or having a kid almost his age.

"Needing to make more money, I realized I would have to get an education and the only way I would be able to pull that off was to get a job with more regular hours so I could go to night school. A friend of mine from high school introduced me to her father who owned a lumber and contractor's supply and was looking for additional accounting help. I was pretty decent with numbers and so with her encouragement, I applied for the job. Miraculously, I got it, probably thanks to the influence of my friend."

"That must've been Irma!" Bertram blurted, happy to have something to contribute.

Norman and Naomi both chuckled. "Yes, that was Irma," she conceded. "Mr. Sykes was an amazing mentor to me, just like he was to Norman… In addition to being flexible while I went to pursue my degree and considerate about my need to parent my child, he taught me the '*Money-Strong Creed*'. At first, I couldn't follow the *Creed* even if I wanted to, mostly because I was so broke. But over time, I passed through one step after another and pretty soon, I was saving money every month and building a very modest little nest egg."

She set her cup and saucer down on the table and scooted back up in her seat.

"Sometime later, after I had gotten my degree in finance and been following the *Creed* for a number of years, the head of Mr. Sykes' accounting team left and he asked me to take over. I had gotten quite comfortable with numbers and knew the business very well, so even though I was scared about the added responsibility, I let him talk me into it."

Bertram was mesmerized, absorbing every word.

"Since I was strictly following the '*Money-Strong Creed*' and had been for a while, the additional salary that came with the bigger job went straight into my investment account, and after a few years the nest egg looked more like it came from an eagle rather than a pigeon, still not huge but much larger than before."

Bertram resisted the urge to barge in to ask questions and Naomi continued.

"Mr. Sykes became ill when I was in my early thirties," she said, "and it was heartbreaking to watch him decline. He fought very hard and battled like the warrior that he was, but in the end it became clear to him that he wasn't going to make it much longer and he came to me to discuss options. After much conversation, he convinced me, and a couple of smaller partners, to buy the business from him. As his illness progressed, I had learned a lot more about managing the other parts of the operation, trying to help keep things running in his absence. It was a stretch to run the whole thing but I knew I had very capable people who had been there forever and that we all trusted each other. So after a few sleepless nights and help from lots of others, we bought the company."

Naomi exuded graciousness and pride, clearly this story and the people in it meant a great deal to her and it energized Bertram just to hear it and the tone in her voice. "That was a little over ten years ago. With a lot of teamwork, that little lumber yard has grown quite a bit and we've all been fortunate enough to have been a part of that story. Most of the original team are the executives and shareholders of the somewhat larger version of Mr. Sykes' vision, and all of them have an ownership stake in our success…" Norman raised a hand, looking like the most overgrown school kid in history. "Yes, Norman?" Naomi asked, giggling.

"Bertram, this woman is selling you a bill of goods. You've heard of Strong and Sons?" he asked, knowing the answer.

"Of course, the big home-improvement stores," Bertram nodded.

"Well, that's what Naomi built out of my father-in-law's little one-shop lumber yard in the sticks," he said with deep respect.

Naomi shook her head, embarrassed at the praise. "That's not a real representation… it was a team. And one that grew up together that made it all happen," she said humbly. "All success is a combination of the right people, diligent work and luck, and somehow this one checked all three boxes. Let me tell you something really important, however; the reason I think that Norman brought you here. I *never* would have been in a position to take a chance and buy Strong and Sons if I hadn't '*saved the difference*' and followed Mr. Sykes' investment rules. Because of the cash I had available, and how the bank viewed my credit risk, I was able to make a dream come true. Without having the little eagle-sized nest egg of savings, no one would have taken a chance on me and I wouldn't have had the option to buy anything. The financial security that I have now and the lifestyle I'm able to afford, all come from that initial plan to '*save the difference*' – a plan which I still follow to this day."

Bertram looked around the room they were in... It, together with the dining room and kitchen area that he could see a sliver of, were larger than the big apartment that he had given up and they only constituted a tiny piece of the overall mansion.

Naomi smiled, knowing instinctively what Bertram was thinking. "Remember, everything scales – or gets bigger or smaller – depending on your income. Your lifestyle can grow, but not before your savings take the lead. I am immensely fortunate, far beyond I ever imagined I would or could ever be. But everything comes back to the '*Money-Strong Creed*' and following it no matter what your income may be. And financial freedom starts with the fifth maxim: '*save the difference*'."

"How did you invest your money originally? I mean, when you first started building your savings," Bertram asked, wondering what kind of knowledge he would need to gain or how complicated Naomi's strategy was.

Naomi stood up and grabbed a tablet that was sitting on the coffee table, handing it and a pen to Bertram. "You ready for it?" she asked playfully, tossing her hair in a way that made her look like a teenager.

He chuckled. "I think so," he said a little nervously.

Naomi asked Bertram for a clean sheet of paper from the tablet she had given him. "Thanks. It's probably not nearly as amazing or even interesting as you might think. There are only two steps." Naomi wrote for a moment in a clear and confident manner, then turned the page toward Bertram. "Here they are:

1. Max out your tax-deferred 401k contribution every month.

    a. Allocate 50% of each contribution to a fund that is all stocks and mimics the S & P 500

    b. Allocate the other 50% of each contribution to a fund that is all bonds, preferably the total bond market

2. Put the rest in a low-cost S & P 500 index fund.

Bertram looked down at the page, then back at Naomi and waited.

"Sorry, that's it," she said. "That's literally all you need to do and all I do to this day." Bertram made a face that said he couldn't quite believe it. "I know, sounds way too easy doesn't it? But that's really all you need to know and I have to say, it kinda worked for me."

Bertram nodded, conceding the point. "I... well, I guess I'm embarrassed to ask this but, what exactly is a 401k?" Bertram asked sheepishly.

"No need to be embarrassed at all, I'm sure most people have no idea what a 401k is but never ask. In simple terms, a 401k is plan set up by your employer that allows you to invest money from your paycheck before any taxes are taken out. In fact, with certain limitations, it allows you to defer all the taxes on those investments until you start withdrawing money, usually after you turn fifty-nine and a half," Naomi explained without a hint of judgment. "What's great is, not only are the associated income taxes on your 401k contributions deferred until later, but so are the taxes on any investment gains you might have over the many years you contribute. There's no tax due until you begin to withdraw money," Naomi elaborated.

"That makes sense. And so what you're saying is, whatever I'm allowed to contribute to my 401k before taxes are taken out of my check, I should take advantage of? I know this sounds silly, but still not sure I understand why?" Bertram had heard this before but wasn't sure he understood it and since Naomi seemed to know what she was talking about, he got past feeling ashamed that he knew very little about the subject of money and investing.

"Yes, that's right. The reason is that tax rates are based upon your annual income. When you are working, your income is high and your tax rates are as well but when you retire, your income and your income tax rates will be much lower. Because you are contributing to the 401k when your income is higher and not getting taxed until you pull out the income after retirement, you will end up paying a whole lot less in taxes. Also, all of your investment returns – meaning the amount your money has grown – will be taxed at an even lower rate called the long-term capital-gains tax," Naomi replied. "Does that make sense?"

Bertram pursed his lips. "I think so. So basically when I contribute out of my paycheck to my 401k, no taxes are taken out. Then much later, when I pull that money out to live on it after I retire, I'm taxed at that time, but since I won't be earning an income anymore, that tax will be very low?" he asked, confirming how he was thinking about it.

"Exactly! Once you are fifty-nine and a half you can pull money out without any penalties and you are taxed at the income tax rate at the time you pull it out," she said, surprised he caught on so quickly. She made an approving nod towards

Norman.

"Ok great, that makes sense. Why would I invest in half stocks and half bonds when I've heard that stocks grow way faster than bonds? Wouldn't I just put it all in stocks?" Bertram wondered.

"The best investment results come when you are consistent and also have something called diversification. All that word means is that you are lowering your risk because all of your eggs are not in one basket. Bonds are important because they can provide stability when the world goes nutso which happens periodically. When stocks struggle, bonds typically do well, balancing out the short-term losses you might have on stocks," Naomi answered. "Also, bonds pay interest. Because those interest payments occur in a 401k, you don't pay taxes on the interest you've earned until you retire, taking advantage of the lower tax rate you have at the time you actually use the money, just like when you contribute from your paycheck."

Bertram seemed to accept Naomi's explanation, wiggling the pen between his index and middle finger. "Wow, that really is pretty simple," he acknowledged.

"Yes, it really is. Just review your 401k's fund choices – they will be somewhat limited by whatever company manages the 401k – and pick your stock fund to be as close as possible to representing the S & P 500 index and your bond fund to mimic the whole US bond market and you'll be done. The fund descriptions will help you with this choice or you can call the administrator of the 401k and they'll help you through it. You just set up the 401k to take fifty cents of every dollar you contribute into the stock fund and fifty cents into the bond fund. Easy peasy, the rest is automatic. Just be sure you only contribute the maximum allowable amount that can be tax-deferred each year, the rest of your invested money will be invested outside of the 401k since there's no tax benefit and you may want access to it before you turn fifty-nine and a half," Naomi expressed.

Norman jumped in. "You can take money out before you turn fifty-nine and a half but it will have a penalty attached. There are certain provisions for hardships but mostly it's a bad idea to touch the 401k until you qualify to tap it without penalty," he elaborated. Naomi affirmed that with a nod.

"I think I get it. Seems fairly straightforward but a little intimidating," Bertram admitted. Naomi's expression showed her compassion. "I remember feeling the same way when I first got rolling. You'll find it isn't as bad as you think," she reassured him.

"In terms of the money I'm investing on my own, why put it in the S & P 500 and what is a low-cost index fund…? I mean I've heard of them but aren't there lots of other choices?" he wondered.

"Sure, there are literally hundreds of mutual fund companies and thousands of mutual funds, index funds, and exchange traded funds. Not to mention tens of thousands of individual companies you could own stock in. All of that makes investing seem confusing when it's actually quite simple. Do you know what the S & P 500 is?" Naomi asked.

"Not exactly…" Bertram said, feeling a little embarrassed.

Naomi nodded. "Most people don't. The S & P 500 is simply an index that tracks the share prices of five hundred large companies. When you hear people talking about 'beating the market' they really mean beating the returns you would have gotten by investing in the S & P 500 index. That's why Mr. Sykes chose it as the way to safely and effectively invest in the stock market. Well, that and the fact that Warren Buffett, the most successful investor who ever lived is so convinced that almost no one can beat the return of the S & P 500 that he directed his investment firm to put ninety percent of his remaining wealth in the S & P 500 after his death." Bertram's eyebrows went up. "Yep, that's right. The winningest stock investor of all time doesn't believe anyone can really beat the market, even though he did it his whole life," Naomi said with some degree of amazement.

Norman decided to give Naomi a little break. "Most people don't realize how much costs and fees can impact the returns they make on their investments. When a share of stock or any type of fund is sold, there are transaction costs paid to all of the people involved. There are brokers on both sides of the transaction, intermediaries, and even fees to the exchanges themselves for facilitating the trade. More importantly, inside most mutual funds, there are large costs associated with operating the fund. This includes paying the fund managers, analysts, and others hefty salaries. In these funds, these costs are passed directly to the investors, meaning that the investors need a much bigger return to pay all of these extra costs and still make money for themselves."

"Wow. So, in most cases, investing in a mutual fund means you pay a lot of extra money that doesn't really help you make more on your investments?" Bertram asked, unsure that he understood completely.

Norman nodded. "Basically, yes. When you put your money in low-cost index funds, such as those run by Vanguard, Fidelity, Schwab, and others, you pay far less in expenses, giving you a much greater potential return. The funny part is, you could pay a lot more fees to funds that invest in the same stocks or bonds, and the only difference is that you'd end up with less money over time," Norman explained.

"Aren't the more expensive funds better somehow? I mean, don't the people who run them know something special that helps them get better results?" Bertram was having trouble figuring out why anyone would pay more for exactly the same thing.

Norman chuckled. "Not really. When it comes to investing, very few people who have ever lived have any sort of a special gift or real expertise. The majority of fund managers never outperform the S & P 500 Index in a single year, much less over time. Not only do they get paid more, they also deliver worse performance. Unfortunately, the only impressive thing about most fund managers is how much they get paid every year," Norman said with a relaxed shrug.

"Dang, Norman, that was pretty good. I'm going to steal that explanation," Naomi observed with pride.

"So basically, these low-cost funds are cheaper to run, which means I'll make more of the money that usually goes to fees for things that don't benefit me?" Bertram offered, summing it up. Naomi and Norman laughed with admiration.

"Kid's a natural," Naomi said.

They spent about a half hour chatting, Bertram trying not to pepper them with too many questions, and said their good-byes, Naomi walking them out to the car.

"Bertram, it was a pleasure to meet you," Naomi said, giving him a hug this time instead of a handshake. "This is my card. Feel free to connect with me if you need something," she said, wandering over to give Norman his good-bye hug. "When do we get to come over for dinner?" she needled her friend. "No one in this house can forget Irma's unbelievable skills!"

Norman smiled in agreement. "Irma would love to see you, Troy, and the kids. I'll check out a few dates and give you a shout." They hugged one last time and pulled slowly out of the motor court, Bertram stealing a last look in the passenger mirror at the fairytale mansion as they pulled out.

The visit to Naomi's was one of the most unexpected experiences of Bertram's life. He had never met such a successful business person, and the fact that she took the adversity of finding herself a single mother and turned that into a home-improvement empire was truly inspiring to him. Not to mention that she was so 'normal' and friendly. Bertram stole a sideways look at his friend and thought that despite the high esteem he already had for Norman, he had probably underestimated him.

As they pulled onto the freeway, Bertram decided to ask a few questions of Norman that had been percolating, hoping he wouldn't look overly nosy. "Can I ask you something personal?" Bertram asked.

"Of course," Norman said, keeping his eyes on the road.

"When Naomi bought Mr. Sykes' business, didn't Irma get a big payday? I mean… it was very successful from what it seems," Bertram asked, wary that he might be overstepping.

"You mean, is Irma filthy rich?" Norman asked, turning briefly to flash a wide smile.

Bertram laughed in relief. "Yeah, that's what I mean," he replied honestly.

"The story is a little complicated. Mr. Sykes mandated a price for the business if it were sold one hundred percent to existing employees or family members far less than it was worth. He did that before he died so it would make it possible for the business to continue to provide a livelihood for the people that built it, so long as they could get the funds put together. It's also important to mention that Mr. Sykes was incredibly generous to the community and he ended up giving over fifty percent of the sale amount to two charities he supported over the years, something his wife and daughters were fully aware of and supportive of. So, although Irma and her siblings had an interest, it was reduced by the family's generosity. The majority of the remaining sales proceeds went to Irma's mom who is still alive and although it was a nice-sized sum, it has been impacted by the increasing amount of care she has needed as she has aged. Irma and her sisters play as much of a role as they can, but they also want her to be as comfortable as possible and are willing to spend every last dime if it ends up being necessary. Irma and the kids will definitely inherit something when her mom does pass on, but it probably won't be a huge amount."

Bertram processed that for a minute. "Mr. Sykes was an amazing guy," he said, thinking about his legacy and his story.

"Certainly was. He knew that if he left too much money to his family, it would take them away from the gift of having made their own way and leave too much room for people to lose the ability to have their own identity and pave a road for themselves. That was a very smart decision and I think has helped the girls a lot… They all have a strong sense of who they are and interests that are meaningful. Yet another thing Mr. Sykes did right," Norman said.

"Did you stay at the company after the sale?" Bertram asked, puzzling through the timing and trying to figure out how Norman missed out on being a part of the Strong and Sons story.

Norman turned and looked at his friend appraisingly. "What, you don't think being a doorman is a noble profession?" he shot back. "You getting fancy again on me?"

Bertram couldn't tell if Norman was joking and he'd never heard a cross word from him, so his response left him speechless for a moment. "I'm… sorry… I didn't…"

Norman laughed hard enough that the car swerved a little.

"I'm just playing with you, Bertram," he said through his laughter, wiping his eyes with one of the handkerchiefs that Bertram had given him for Christmas. "Oh man, that was funny."

Bertram was just relieved that he hadn't ticked him off and chuckled politely to express it.

"Let's go hang at the park for a few and I'll tell you that story too if you'd like."

Norman pulled into one of the parking spots at the tennis-court area of the park across from the building and shut off the car. They climbed out and wandered over to a free bench overlooking the lawn. There were lots of people and families enjoying the warmer than typical early spring day, playing games, picnicking, or quietly reading a book, and it was fun to see everyone having a great time.

"Good call, Norman," Bertram said as they sat down, sounds of squealing children, people laughing, and solidly hit tennis balls filtering through the air.

"Yes, I love this time of year," Norman said, settling his big frame on the wooden bench. "When Mr. Sykes died, it was worse than when I lost my own father. Don't get me wrong, I loved my dad but we just didn't have much of a relationship, especially when I was younger. He made some bad choices and didn't play a huge role in my life. Mr. Sykes, on the other hand, taught me many things like what it meant to have a work ethic and to be a man of integrity and character. I loved him deeply. I also loved Sykes Supply – what it was called back then – it felt like home to me and the people who worked there, including Naomi, were my best friends. It was actually fun to go to work."

Norman paused to watch an acrobatic dog in astonishment as it leaped in the air to consistently catch a frisbee at atmospheric heights. Bertram and Norman looked at each other in disbelief, mutually amazed.

"After Mr. Sykes passed, I began to feel differently. It felt like work for the first time since I had joined the company twelve years before. Irma and I were expecting our first baby and we were both saddened by the fact that Mr. Sykes would never meet that baby. Everything around me, even my own wife, reminded me of him and the fact that he was gone. Naomi coaxed me into slowly getting my mojo back and I put some money into the company so they could settle the sale with his estate, more to help my friends to complete the sale than because I had any passion for it. In addition, Irma elected to take half of her small interest in shares so the new owners wouldn't have to come up with the additional cash, so between the two of us, we owned a little piece of the new company."

"Is that when you changed the name – when you guys bought it from Mr. Sykes' estate?" Bertram asked.

"To be clear, the sale was all Naomi. Man, that woman is a force. She arranged the financing, organized the legal team – really did everything since most of the rest of us didn't know much about the operations or financial side of the business. We were just lucky enough to have followed the '*Money-Strong Creed*' and have a little money saved. She had never done any of this before either, but she was smart, tireless and had a vision of what she thought we could build.

"One day we were sitting around after the warehouse closed and talking about things, just hanging out after a long day, something we did fairly often. Naomi said that she had been thinking and that it might be powerful to rename the company in a way that paid deference to its history but might be more catchy as we grew. There were mixed reactions to the idea and everyone chatted about it for a while. Then, one of the loaders, a big scary-looking guy we all called Boxer who had been there since before I joined, who worked like a devil and barely ever said a word, bellowed, 'How about '*Strong and Sons*?' We looked at him for a second before Naomi squealed,

'I love it! Mr. Sykes taught us to be *'Money-Strong'* and we're like his sons and daughters. It's perfect!!' And that was pretty much it for the name. It really was a good name since literally every single person that invested in the new company had learned how to be *'Money-Strong'* from Mr. Sykes, which was the only reason any of them could have ever afforded to put money into the sale in the first place. Naomi was also clear that our biggest customers were contractors and a powerful masculine-sounding name might play well in other places."

A tennis ball bounced over a few feet away from where they were sitting; obviously a wayward traveler from the courts behind them. Bertram jumped up to throw it back, easily pitching it the thirty yards or so necessary to get it back to its owner who yelled a thank you in response.

"Man, you still have quite an arm," Norman noted.

Bertram shrugged humbly and sat back down. "What happened from there?" he asked, not wanting the story to end.

"We all kept working and slowly I started to feel normal. Irma and I had Stella and that was hard but fantastic. Naomi asked me to run the whole warehouse because I knew how it all operated and all the employees respected me. I resisted because I liked filling orders with the customers and having those relationships too…but finally I took the job. It was then that I knew I had to do something else… it was just time. I was really impressed with the company's rapid growth, but the growth took me away from what I liked to do every day and my heart just wasn't in it. Since I had plenty of money saved, I decided to figure out what I wanted to do next and leave Strong and Sons once I had a clear direction."

"Wasn't Irma nervous about you leaving? I mean you guys had a new baby and needed the income, didn't you?" Bertram asked, surprised that Norman would leave such a great opportunity.

Norman shrugged. "We still had a pretty good amount

saved from all of those years of '*saving the difference*' and I knew I wouldn't have much of a gap in income, even if I didn't find something that paid very well. We made the decision together." He shook his head. "She always supported me and I supported her. Then and now."

Bertram waited for him to continue. "What did you eventually decide to do?" he prodded.

"Oh, it took a while. I thought about a bunch of different things but came up with property management as one that seemed to fit. I studied more about it and eventually got a job in a small commercial property -management firm to learn the business. I was there about five years and learned a great deal about how to do it both right and wrong. I started thinking it would be cool to buy a building and see if I could use my skills to turn it around – you know, remodel it and get new tenants, that kind of thing. Commercial real estate was going through a tough time and I could buy things really cheaply but I didn't have that much money and wasn't really willing to take much risk. Luckily for me, around that time Strong and Sons went public. Between Irma and I we had a tidy little sum and I decided to use some of it to buy my first building."

Bertram stared at his friend, knowing what the punchline was going to be before he got there, feeling like a total idiot that he hadn't figured it out before. Norman felt his friend's eyes boring into him and stopped.

"What is it, Bertram? You ok?" Norman asked, puzzled.

"You aren't the doorman. You own the building, don't you?!" Bertram gushed, like he'd just solved the mystery of the *Pink Panther*.

Norman laughed at his friend's zeal, impressed with his powers of deduction. "Yes, yes," he said nodding. "I, and my partners, own the building. But, I'm also the doorman… I do that because I love getting to know the tenants and for the first two years, every time I buy a building, I do something similar to be sure I understand what the tenants need and how they feel about the place," Norman admitted. "Let's face it, at the end of the day, the buildings are only as good as the tenants think they are."

Bertram was still shocked, even though he had been the one to make the discovery, and was trying to let it all sink in. Norman went on to explain a little more of the story – how Mrs. Winslow had helped him finance all of the buildings, how many of the initial '*Money-Strong*' team of Strong and Sons investors were also partners in the buildings, and how he volunteered time and money to teach others to become '*Money-Strong*' – painting a picture that became instantly obvious to Bertram in retrospect.

They sat together for a few more minutes, soaking up the sun, enjoying the sounds of spring, and the pleasure of hanging quietly with a friend after a very big day.

By late May, it was clear that Allen wasn't going to beat his illness. The chemo hadn't been successful at achieving remission and he had made the decision not to pursue further treatment in an attempt to enjoy some of the time he had left. Bertram was now making the trip out every weekend and even though Allen was very tired and sick from all of the medication, their visits were always worth the effort. Allen opened up about all sorts of things in his life, including his experience in the Iraq war as an infantryman, and they shared a level of detail that would have seemed impossible four months earlier.

Gina was starting to set up the spare bedroom on the

ground floor as a spot where Allen could stay as things got worse, making it easier for him than going up the stairs to bed and for people who might administer care over time. She bought an assisted chair and a few other items but held off on a hospital bed, knowing that the kids would be extremely affected by it and hoping to put off the impact of the reality of his condition as long as possible.

As the disease began to get the better of Allen, Bertram helped Gina to do everything possible to make him comfortable. The progression of its impact was far faster than anyone expected, leading the doctors to believe he was further along than they thought when he was initially diagnosed. Within a short period of time, Allen couldn't get himself up to use the restroom and didn't have much of an appetite, even for foods he loved.

One night, Bertram was sitting in the motorized recliner by Allen's bed after dinner. Allen had dozed off for a bit and Bertram was reading an article on his phone when he was startled by Allen's raspy voice.

"Hey, Bertram," Allen croaked out. Bertram stood up and went to his brother's bedside.

His brother reached out his hand from under the covers and Bertram took it, first with one hand and then with both. Allen looked at his brother and smiled slowly. "I've loved getting this time with you," he said, obviously struggling to get out the words. "Thank you for being here… It's made this whole crummy thing so much better…" He nodded very slightly and then shut his eyes for a moment.

Bertram was openly crying, unable to respond. "I love you too, big brother," he finally managed and they sat there holding hands until Allen drifted back to sleep.

His visit with Allen still hanging heavily against the inside of his chest, Bertram decided to grab a few groceries before heading back to the city, hoping the brightly lit bustling energy of the supermarket would provide enough distraction for him. He sat for a moment in his car to be sure he had all of his emotional hatches strapped back down and cruised through the market, finding most of what he needed for the week. Bertram didn't cook often but he did like to throw together a big salad or something else easy, usually frozen, so he could eat at home and '*save the difference*'. All of the money he used to spend on take out and dine-in rapidly added to his growing nest egg and it felt good to watch his investment-account balance build every two weeks. With everything that had been going on in his life, it was gratifying to make progress at something and feel a little success, even if it was incremental.

Bertram was just rounding the corner towards the checkout stands when he almost bumped smack into someone. It was Bessie. They hadn't seen each other in a number of weeks and she looked tan and relaxed, her face opening from slight alarm and confusion to genuine surprise and pleasure.

"Bertram!" she chirped, giving him a big hug which he happily returned.

"Sorry I almost mowed you over," he said, apologizing for his high-speed cart maneuvers.

"No problem," she laughed. "Are you staying in town?" she asked, looking at the relatively domestic contents of his basket.

"Nah, just saw Allen, actually, and…" His face clouded and Bessie touched him on the arm.

"Why don't you get checked out and we can chat for a bit?" she suggested, hoping she could provide some comfort. Bertram nodded and thanked her and she followed him to the car, leaving her own cart half full at the front where one of the cashiers kindly offered to hold on to it.

Bertram turned the car on to keep them cool and spilled the whole thing out at once. He hadn't yet told anyone about how difficult it had been to help care for his brother or how rewarding the time they had together had been. For the second time in their long acquaintance, Bertram couldn't hold back his emotions, tears streaming down his face for much of the conversation while he pushed through to get it out. Bessie cried too, providing the comfort she could and knowing a different version of his current reality. When he had gotten purged of all of his observations and at least some of the feelings he'd been harboring, he sat back against the seat cushion and stared out the windshield.

After a time, he turned to look at Bessie who had her knees tucked up under her and her head propped up on an elbow facing him.

"I'm really proud of you for being there for Allen. It says a lot about who you are," she said. "You really have become an amazing man... I wish..." She drifted off. Bertram turned to face her. "I think I owe you an apology," she said carefully. "I guess I want you to know that I'm sorry. I wish that things could have been different... I do... I love you, Bertram. But I think that the planets didn't align for us and even though I love you, and probably always will, I just can't bring myself to... It's just not meant to be between us. I don't feel like I said that before clearly, probably because I wasn't sure myself. I... I'm sorry."

Bertram seemed to accept the news with understanding, almost as if was speaking to someone else. "I'm not surprised. It's not as if you haven't tried to tell me that a few times." He smiled to let Bessie know he was ok. "I guess that this is what love really looks like. It's not the romantic stuff you see on TV or even the way you feel about somebody... It's what you do when someone needs you the most, even if they don't recognize it at the time," Bertram suggested.

Bessie smiled and gave a small nod, fighting back tears.

"Thanks for being here for me," Bertram said emotionally. "I don't think I could have done this day alone." He grabbed both of her hands in his and leaned his forehead against hers as her tears fell freely, sharing a moment of quiet that they both seemed to need.

On the day of Allen's funeral, Bertram dressed in his best suit and tie, despite the humid summer weather, and prepared to say goodbye. He had been back and forth multiple times at the very end and had helped Gina arrange the Episcopalian funeral service and manage some other details. He had become very close to her and the girls and knew that he needed to be strong for them, even though he didn't feel all that strong himself. "One foot in front of the other..." he said to himself as he walked out the door.

Norman happened to be at his regular post talking to a delivery person when Bertram got to the lobby and he broke away to say, "Hello". They had spoken regularly over the past few weeks so Norman didn't say much, just folded his friend into his large wingspan and held him for a moment. "Well, at least you look fine," he said admiringly to Bertram who welcomed the comic relief.

They chatted quietly for a moment and Norman suggested that they get together for dinner at his house. "Irma has been asking about you and we'd love to get together when we can sit outside while we can still enjoy the weather."

"Sure, that would be really great... I could use some of Irma's amazing food in my life right now." Norman nodded in understanding and they picked a date a couple of weeks out.

As Bertram walked to the garage entrance, Norman called after him. "Hey, Bertram, don't forget your plaque – I believe we have some business to attend to there," he said officiously.

"Oh wow, yeah, that's awesome. Will do," Bertram said, having to think for a second to remember that the final line of the *Creed* was still missing.

"Why don't you come by a half-hour early and we'll do it together?" Norman suggested.

"Ok, sounds great. Thanks, Norman," Bertram said, thankful to have something pleasant to look forward to after a hard few months.

Bertram looked at his '*Money-Strong Creed*' plaque, thinking how amazingly different his financial life was today from just over a year ago. Not only did he have no debt, a month of emergency money, and a rapidly growing investment account, he also had a completely new way of looking at life. His relationship with his parents had never been stronger, the death of his brother bringing them closer together and deepening their relationship.

He continued to go to Weaver almost every weekend and more often than not, he'd spend the night with his folks, usually enjoying a simple meal together before sitting around the kitchen table and chatting until late. Sometimes one of his other siblings would join them and other times it was just the three of them. They talked about everything and nothing and Bertram enjoyed it either way. He felt lucky to have figured out how much these relationships mattered to him and to be in a position to take advantage of the realization.

Bertram also had started to see the impact of his daily decisions to '*spend less*', watching as all of the money he used to spend on minimum payments, a larger apartment, a fancier car and trendier meals began to go to work in his investment account. He had gotten to the point where he really thought about every dollar he spent, consciously deciding where his money should go and why, being intentional about his choices.

Investing was new to him but he had done exactly what

Naomi had suggested and couldn't believe that he'd already started to make some gains in both his 401k and his portfolio of low-cost funds. Bertram knew that if he kept living this way, choices and possibilities that he couldn't envision would open up to him and he was very grateful for his friendship with Norman.

He couldn't help but smile as he tucked the plaque under his arm and grabbed the orchid he had bought for Irma, feeling almost normal for the first time in many months.

Bertram greeted Irma at the door as she gave him a big hug, happily taking the orchid off his hands and directing him in to find Norman who was already back in the shop.

Norman was polishing something on the grinder when Bertram came in, so Bertram got a chance to look around the shop unattended. It was a much larger and better-equipped shop than Bertram expected, complete with compressed-air stations and commercial-grade tools for both woodworking and metalworking. Everything was extremely well-organized and labeled; there was not one hint of clutter anywhere. More astoundingly, Bertram couldn't believe how clean the shop was, given how much wood and other material had been cut, shaped, pounded and filed there. The shop floor gleamed in such a way that it almost looked liquid and even the stationary tools like the table saw and miter station didn't have any noticeable collection of sawdust anywhere.

Bertram was shaking his head in disbelief when Norman surprised him from behind by putting one of his catcher's mitt-sized hands on his shoulder. They gave each other a hug with a few back slaps.

"How are you hanging in there, Bertram?" Norman said, taking a step back and looking at his friend with concern.

"Honestly, not too bad at all," he said, happy to be able to report a sincere and positive answer.

Norman nodded appreciatively. "That's real good. You've

had a few things coming at you, that's for sure." He grabbed a hose that was clipped inconspicuously into the wall and using ceiling tracks, maneuvered it over to where he had been working, flicking a switch on the wall and bringing a vacuum system to life that sounded like the growl of an angry tiger.

"So that's how you do it," Bertram said, feeling like Norman had pulled the sword from the stone.

"What's that?" Norman asked, confused.

"Keep this place cleaner than an operating room," Bertram retorted. "It's unbelievable."

"Well, all those years working for Mr. Sykes drilled into me a reverence for a clean shop. He used to say, 'Remember, the showroom is for customers and our customers are choosing to come to our house. You wouldn't leave your house a big mess when company is coming over, would you?' He believed early on that home-improvement customers would increasingly include the woman of the house and he didn't want to disappoint them or make them feel unwelcome," Norman explained.

"He was sure right about that," Bertram observed.

"Let's take a look at that plaque of yours, young man," Norman said with enthusiasm.

Bertram handed him the '*Money-Strong Creed*', a little nervous that Norman might ask him to etch the final maxim since he had never done anything like that in his life.

Norman waived him over to a machine with a small keyboard and color interface. "You want to do the honors?" he asked, motioning to the keyboard and opening the plexiglass top of something that resembled a small space shuttle with a stainless-steel arm hovering over its interior. "Just type in the words and this fancy little beast will do the rest." Norman gushed like a kid stepping back to admire a complicated model airplane that took a month to assemble.

Bertram did as instructed and the machine quickly and

quietly lasered the words in exactly the right spot. Norman then entered a few quick pecks into the keyboard and about fifteen seconds later, Bertram's name and the date were inscribed in the lower right corner. Pulling the plaque out of its torture chamber, he polished it with a microfiber cloth and held it up for them both to admire.

THE MONEY-STRONG CREED

Adjust your expectations

Spend less

Obey the One-Month Rule

Eliminate debt

Save the difference

"Looks good, right?" Norman asked, already knowing the answer.

"It's awesome," Bertram agreed.

They tidied up the shop and walked the stone path to the pool area where a smoke pit was creating some sort of magic that made Bertram salivate. "Oh man, that smells good," he said, instantly feeling hungry.

"Yup, I've been roasting some brisket for my famous sandwiches... Irma isn't the only one in this place with some game," he said, thrusting his chin out and laughing at himself. "Wait until you try her French potato salad... You've never had anything like it in your life..."

Norman threw his arm over Bertram's shoulder and they made their way into the kitchen, walking together in the relaxed way that good friends with some history and a lot of respect often do.

Norman went to pull some drinks out of the extra refrigerator in the garage and told Bertram he didn't need help, so Bertram went into the house through the open slider in the great room before rounding the corner to the kitchen. He was surprised to bump into Naomi who was at the kitchen counter, laughing and chatting with Irma while popping a few honey-roasted peanuts, looking completely radiant.

Naomi smiled broadly and gave him a hug in greeting and noticed the plaque which was still under his arm.

"So, what phase are you in?" she asked conspiratorially.

Bertram, in a rare moment of embarrassment, shared that he had just graduated.

"Oh that's fantastic, good for you! Wait until you see how your life changes," Naomi said, speaking from experience.

Bertram excused himself to use the restroom and was walking back towards the kitchen when the doorbell rang. "Irma, do you want me to grab that?" Bertram asked, since he was just past the foyer area.

"Thanks, hon, that would be great," Irma yelled back, her hands otherwise occupied with the dressing for her potato salad.

Bertram opened the door. He had to do a double-take, thinking for a split second that Naomi had gone out to the car to get something she had forgotten.

"Hi?" the Naomi lookalike said tentatively, with that impossible-to-resist smile.

Bertram, attempting to compose himself, stammered a, "Hello," but not much else. Upon meeting Naomi he thought to himself that he didn't think anyone could possibly be more magnetic or beautiful, and now had just been proven wrong.

"Do you think I can I come in?" the clone asked with a short giggle.

"Oh, jeez, yes, sorry," Bertram said, stepping out of the way and coming back to planet earth. "I'm sorry but you look so much like…"

"My mom?" the woman interrupted.

"I'm Monica, Naomi's oldest," she said, extending a hand and giving Bertram a solid handshake.

"Hi, I'm an idiot, and you can call me Bertram," he said, recovering a bit from his initial shock and awe. She laughed and he showed her in and brought her to the kitchen area where there were big hugs all around.

Bertram, still feeling awkward, went out to check on Norman who had deposited the drinks in the refrigerator and then headed out to tend to his brisket. He found Norman muscling the brisket on the smoker to give it just a few more minutes before letting it settle. Taking off one of his barbeque mitts which looked big enough to house a mid-sized car, he looked up briefly at Bertram, chuckled, and then fiddled with the vents on the smoker with his still-gloved hand.

"What's funny?" Bertram asked.

"I see you've met Monica," he said, still amused.

"What… How… Why do you say that?" Bertram said, flustered.

Norman stood up and shed the other glove, smiling with both of his eyebrows raised. "Well, either that or you got hit by an asteroid. I used to see that look on people's faces when they first met Naomi. I guess it runs in the family."

Bertram conceded the point with a shake of the head, causing Norman to bend over with laughter. The two men stood there, Norman smiling contentedly while waiting for the smoker to finish its job and Bertram trying, moderately successfully, to reorient himself.

After dinner at the teak dining table by the pool, they all hung out for a while attempting to digest their meal.

"Man, am I stuffed," Norman said. "I probably shouldn't have had that extra sandwich." Everyone giggled, commiserating with his position.

Naomi's husband, Troy, and her two younger kids who had arrived a little after dinner started were headed to the pool for an after-meal swim, everyone else marveling at their ability to move, much less maintain their energy and interest for physical activity. The kids had arrived still wearing their baseball uniforms and exchanged them for swimming trunks almost immediately.

"Those two are pretty hilarious," Monica said. "They just never stop. And somehow Troy keeps up with them," she marveled.

Everyone smiled, content to watch Troy and the kids horse around while they worked up enough room to pay proper homage to Irma's summer-berry crumble, which was cooling and almost ready for action.

At some point, Naomi went to sit by the pool and Irma and Norman went to get coffee and dessert ready, leaving Bertram and Monica by themselves. They shared a few details of their lives, finding that they had more in common than either would have expected. Monica was a student athlete in college, playing volleyball all four years of her time at the University of Texas, but unlike Bertram, had been a bit of a math whizz and didn't struggle with school. She also decided to stay closer to home even though her initial career path was leading her towards New York City and a fast-lane life in the financial world. Her mom was her best friend and she didn't want to miss playing a part in her younger half-brothers' lives, worried that she'd get sucked up in the competitive energy of the city and not have time for other interests.

"What other interests – other than your family, I mean – were you worried you'd miss out on?" Bertram asked curiously.

"Well…" Monica paused as if she were unsure of herself, something that seemed completely impossible to Bertram given how clearly amazing she was. "You might think it's kind of weird. I've been working on a financial literacy program for school-aged kids, using the '*Money-Strong Creed*' as the basis of it. Watching my mom go from a struggling single mother who could barely juggle everything in her financial life to a business mogul left a major impression. As I got a little older, she taught me the *Creed* and I've always wondered if you could teach it to kids earlier in life, what kind of a difference it would make…"

Bertram nodded enthusiastically, asking more questions, clearly very interested in her idea.

"I'm not sure that I'm quite ready yet, but I'm going to leave my job as an analyst sometime in the next few months and focus full time on this project," she shared, surprising herself at the disclosure.

"That's really cool," Bertram said with real admiration. "Keep me up to speed…"

At that moment, the crumble, coffee and tea arrived and everyone started to hover around like bees in a hive. Bertram and Monica gave each other a little smile that signaled they both enjoyed the conversation, and then joined in as everyone found room in their too-stuffed bodies to fit a few bites of crumble with homemade butter-pecan gelato.

Nothing but the sounds of contentment and the calls of crickets floated through the air as everyone quietly took in the end of a near-perfect summer evening as the last wisps of sunlight were exchanged for the glow of fireflies.

A little less than a year later, Bertram was packing up his office late on a Thursday night. He had isolated Thursday as the day he worked late, using it to catch up on paperwork and handle things that required more attention since the rhythm of his typical day was often interrupted with phone calls, emails, and text messages. It looked like he was going to have a very good year and was pleased with the progress, but he wanted to insure they had enough in the pipeline to blow through their annual objective and he still felt like there was room for improvement.

On his way out the door, he noticed that someone else's office light was still burning further down the hallway and decided to wander down and check it out. Bertram wasn't used to seeing anyone else around the office this late and was curious as to who might be burning the midnight oil.

"Knock, knock," Bertram said peering in the office doorway.

Martin Harden, one of the newer people on Bertram's team, was at his desk staring intently at his computer screen, absently patting down and smoothing his longish brown hair. He jumped a little when Bertram spoke, thinking that he was the only person left on the floor.

"Sorry to startle you, Marty, everything ok?"

Bertram had inherited Marty from another regional manager when the company shifted territories late last year and hadn't gotten to know him well, but early indications were that he was hard working, conscientious and a team player, someone Bertram thought he could develop.

"Hi, Bertram. Yes thanks, everything's fine," Marty said, not very convincingly.

Bertram sat down in one of the two metal frame chairs across the desk from Marty. "Are you sure? If everything's fine, what is a guy with a beautiful wife and an adorable daughter doing sitting in his office looking like a sad sack at seven-thirty?" Bertram chided, flicking his head toward the many photographs in the bookcase behind Marty's chair.

Marty rolled back from the desk in his chair looking a bit

like he was deciding whether he wanted to take offense or to open up. After a moment, his shoulders slumped a little and he looked down at his hands which had settled on the desk. "Honestly, I'm trying to figure out how to tell my family that we can't go to Disneyworld next month like we'd been planning," he said, obviously distraught over having to share this news with his wife and daughter. "My daughter, Phoebe, has been looking forward to the trip for over a year and it's been booked since December. She'll be… heartbroken," he explained.

Bertram listened patiently and intently.

"The thing is…" Marty seemed uncomfortable sharing personal details with his boss, especially a new one who was a few years younger than himself. "It's that we can't really afford it," he said, unable to hide his shame.

"Oh, that's really awful," Bertram said. "Has something changed or was it just a splurge that sounded good until it got closer to reality?" Bertram asked, looking genuinely concerned.

Seeing the lack of judgement on Bertram's face, Marty relaxed a bit and shared the whole story. Apparently, when he moved over from the northeastern territory late last year, he'd gotten a little bump in pay. He and his wife, Gloria, had used that extra salary to qualify for a loan on a home that was considerably larger than their place outside of Boston and had found themselves over-budget furnishing the additional space. After the move, Gloria, who had left a good job in Boston, looked for work for a few months without results, and eventually took a job that paid quite a bit less than the position she had left behind. To make matters worse, during the time she was job-hunting, they'd burned through what was left of their cash and were running on fumes. Things weren't desperate… yet. But there was no way they could afford to load a twenty-thousand-dollar vacation on their credit card at this point, given their situation.

Bertram listened with compassion to Marty's story, relating deeply to the feeling of stress and anxiety he was going through. "Man, I totally understand where you are, probably more than you know…"

Bertram told him about his own story of financial distress in some detail, how his ego and lifestyle had helped him to build an unmanageable level of debt and financial obligation and how he felt trapped and hopeless. He summed the story up on a hopeful note by sharing the fact that with some significant help and hard work, he was able to do a complete one eighty-degree turn in just over a year and now lived completely without money worries.

Marty, pleased that his boss was willing to share his own story in such gory detail, seemed astounded about the turnaround. "That's amazing, Bertram, and I would love to make that happen in my own situation… It just seems so far away from reality right now. We're so buried in debt and monthly obligations, I can't imagine being totally free from it, much less have some money saved. Do you think there's any way I could do something similar?" he asked, doubt hanging heavily in his voice.

"Absolutely," Bertram said confidently. He then stood up while motioning Marty to follow him and they both walked towards his office. "Well, you're not going to believe this, but I got my financial life together solely and only because of the doorman at my apartment complex," he said, walking over to the credenza and picking up his '*Money-Strong Creed*' plaque and handing it to Marty.

Marty looked confused. "You got financial advice from… your doorman?" he asked quizzically, while looking over the plaque. "This plaque is how you turned your finances around?"

THE MONEY-STRONG CREED

Adjust your expectations

Spend less

Obey the One-Month Rule

Eliminate debt

Save the difference

Bertram laughed. "Not exactly the plaque itself. Let me tell you about the most amazing doorman you'll ever meet and how he changed my life, and might just change yours…"

———

THE END

Acknowledgements

For many people, the topic of personal finance can be boring, intimidating, confusing or even embarrassing. In some cases, it may be all of these at once. This book is an attempt at simplifying the basics of personal finance and making it possible for anyone with an income to make better financial choices. The decisions, efforts and transformations of the lives of the many friends, family members, colleagues, and clients I've had the good fortune of being associated with provided plenty of inspiration to write it, and their struggles, experiences and triumphs made the whole thing possible.

While it's impossible to list all of the people in my life that have had an impact on the contents of this endeavor, there are a few that deserve special mention. I'm particularly indebted to my friends, Curt Berrien, Janet Berrien, and Alan Steremberg for reading multiple drafts and making excellent suggestions with kindness and care. I was also fortunate enough to have my father, Larry Miller, read both early and later versions and provide feedback that helped me course correct the original concept. My team on the other side of the pond, Lisa Edwards and Clare Baggaley, lent their brilliant editorial support and design skills to the book, transforming it into something readable and beautiful to look at.

To my daughter Lindsay, her husband Andrew, and their perfect babies Paxton and Addy, your perspectives helped to solidify many of the fundamental concepts, while the smiles of your children made some of the toughest writing days seem a little easier. Finally, a mammoth thank you to my wife and best friend, Janet Miller, who read every word of each flailing attempt and used her love, wisdom and skill to encourage me to make this a better book – and me a better person.

Made in the USA
Monee, IL
07 July 2026

56550197R00118